TRUTH

THE LIES WE'VE BEEN TOLD

Written by

JARED MILLER

https://www.JaredMillerOfficial.com

Skinny Brown Dog Media
http://www.SkinnyBrownDogMedia.com

Published by Skinny Brown Dog Media
Atlanta, GA/Punta del Este, Uruguay
http://www.SkinnyBrownDogMedia.com

Copyright © 2022 Jared Miller
https://www.JaredMillerOfficial.com

Distributed by Skinny Brown Dog Media

Design and composition by Skinny Brown Dog Media
Cover Design by Skinny Brown Dog Media

Cover Design by Skinny Brown Dog Media
Library of Congress Cataloging-in-Publication Data Print

eBook ISBN: 978-1-957506-29-6
Hardback ISBN: 978-1-957506-28-9
paperback ISBN: 978-1-957506-27-2

Every effort has been made to locate and credit the copyright owners of material and quotes in this book. If any sources have not been credited, please call this to our attention, and we will make every effort to correct this in future printings.

Dedication

This book is dedicated to my sons, Grayson and Owen.
Your lives are proof of the miraculous nature of Truth.

Acknowledgments

I would like to thank:

My family: Dad, Mom, Paige, Jon, Skylar, and all the Miller and Perkins family. Thank you for your love and support of this book and its message.

Eric G. Reid: Your guidance on this book journey, professionally and personally, has stretched, challenged, and grown me as an author and a man. Thank you!

Dennis LaRue: Your impact on my life over the last year as my coach has been priceless. I am better because of you.

Jose Escobar: In such a short time, you have made such a significant impact on my life through your servant leadership. You have supported me beyond my expectations. I am grateful

Von Won: After all these years, we did it. Your push to create a song together is precisely what I needed. *Truth* is more than a book or a song. It's the message that the world needs to hear.

Pastors Randy and Renee Clark: Thank you for your love, support, and pastoral leadership in my life all these years. So much of who I'm becoming is because of your influence in my life.

Courtney: Thank you for giving me two of God's greatest gifts: Grayson and Owen. Thank you for being such an incredible mother to our sons. And thank you for forcing me to face the Truth; it has changed me for the better.

TRUTH: The Lies We've Been Told
Jared Miller

Dedication iii

Acknowledgments v

Introduction 1

Chapter 1: What is Truth? 3

- Different Types of Truth 6
  - Empirical Truth vs. Convenient Truth................... 7
  - Absolute Truth vs. Relative Truth 9
  - Objective Truth vs. Subjective Truth................... 11
  - Moral Objectivism vs. Moral Relativism.............. 13
  - Normative Truth vs. Complex Truth................. 14
- Feed Me the Truth 16

Chapter 2: Why We Need Truth 19

- Wisdom for Today.. 22
- Does It Matter What I Believe? 25
- The Object of Belief vs. the Act of Belief 28
- Investigate the Truth... 29
- Truth Has a Voice 30
- The Physiology of Hearing 32
- The McGurk Effect 33

Chapter 3: What Influences Our Acceptance
of Something As Truth? 37

- The Voices Behind You: Past Influences 41
- Back to the Future 42
- The Voices in Front of You: Future
  Influences 51

Chapter 4: How Truth Is Built 53

- What Makes a Strong Foundation? 56
- The Voices Around You: Relational
  Influences 59
- The Voices Inside You: The Influence
  of Self-Talk 71
- Truth Filters 73
- We Want the Truth 75

Chapter 5: Divine Truth 77

- Reasons Divine Truth Exists 83
- Divine Truth Must Be Tested 84
- Divine Truth Must Be Transformative 101
- Divine Truth Must Be Transcendent 106
- Divine Truth's Defining Moment 108
- What Does Divine Truth Mean to You? 111

A Personal Invitation To Know Divine Truth 117

About the Author 121

Congratulations! 123

One Last Thing 125

Introduction

Truth and purpose are hot topics these days. It seems everyone is trying to figure out what their truth is and why they were put on the earth. As a leader, I have seen an entire generation searching and hungry to know what's truth and what's fake. You can't seem to shake the feeling that something is missing. You're feeling a little lost and frustrated, which creates a lot of guilt because, you think, *What more could I possibly want?!* You want clarity. You want to know exactly who you are and what you want in life. You want to know what your purpose is, and you want to be living in alignment with it every single day. You want direction. You want clear steps on how to find your purpose and, more importantly, how to bring it to life. You want a clear, easy-to-follow plan (that you'll actually stick to!). And you want to create a positive impact. You're here to make a difference in the world.

Trust me, I understand. We live in an age when truth has become increasingly subjective and perspectival. What is truth for me may not be truth to you. As a result, the whole notion of absolute truth has died, and, in terms of the conventional definition, there is no more truth. All that is left are varying points of view. "True

1

truth" matters. It always does, and it always will. Only an understanding of why truth matters and defining "true truth" can give you confidence that your life has a purpose.

Truth: The Lies We've Been Told started as a self-reflection to understand what "truth" meant and how that truth was shaping my decisions, actions, and character. As I talked to others about what I was discovering about the idea of truth, I realized others were also struggling with similar questions regarding the truths that they had allowed to shape their lives, families, and businesses.

I felt called to find clarity on how influence, trust, and truth were affecting my life and shaping my leadership. *Truth: The Lies We've Been Told* resulted from the clarity and understanding I found and was written as a guide for others seeking to establish a foundation of TRUTH in their life and leadership.

As you read *Truth: The Lies We've Been Told*, you'll learn that truth and purpose are something you already carry within you and that they just need to be uncovered and reignited. Together, we'll explore what truth is, how truth is built, and why it is so hard to see the truth in today's world. We will also explore the reason behind the difficulty in finding your purpose and casting a vision to become a person of purpose and influence. *Truth: The Lies We've Been Told* will help you find that great calling you are here to fulfill.

Chapter 1
What Is Truth?

"All truths are easy to understand once they are discovered; the point is to discover them"

\- Galileo Galilei

If you've seen the movie *A Few Good Men*, you may recall this scene:

> Lieutenant Kaffee: Colonel Jessep! Did you order the Code Red?!
>
> Judge Randolph: You don't have to answer that question!
>
> Colonel Jessup: I'll answer the question. You want answers?
>
> Lieutenant Kaffee: I think I'm entitled to them.
>
> Colonel Jessup: You want answers?!
>
> Lieutenant Kaffee: I want the truth!
>
> Colonel Jessup: You can't handle the truth! Son, we live in a world that has walls, and those walls have to be guarded by men with guns. Who's gonna do it?

3

You? You, Lieutenant Weinberg? I have a greater responsibility than you can possibly fathom…you weep for Santiago, and you curse the Marines. You have that luxury. You have the luxury of not knowing what I know—that Santiago's death, while tragic, probably saved lives, and my existence, while grotesque and incomprehensible to you, saves lives.

You don't want the truth because deep down, in places you don't talk about at parties, you want me on that wall—you need me on that wall. We use words like "honor," "code," and "loyalty." We use these words as the backbone of a life spent defending something. You use them as a punch line. I have neither the time nor the inclination to explain myself to a man who rises and sleeps under the blanket of the very freedom that I provide and then questions the manner in which I provide it. I would rather that you just said, "thank you," and went on your way. Otherwise, I suggest you pick up a weapon and stand the post.

When Jack Nicholson spoke these famous words in the movie *A Few Good Men*, the line "You can't handle the truth!" became an instant classic, permanently etched in American pop culture. There is great wisdom in this short quote, as it expresses an important reality: Most people can't handle the truth about many things, and many of our problems in life spring from our avoidance of the more difficult truths of life. You have probably heard the saying that success leaves clues. These clues are universal truths that we observe successful people following that provide an example of what to do if we want to be successful. Universal truths are truths or beliefs we accept as being accurate and unchangeable. Some truths are more apparent; for example, humans need to breathe air to survive, gravity makes things fall, and water is wet. Another truth is what I call "The Rule of 168." There are only 168 hours in the week, and your success and happiness in life are determined by how you choose to invest your 168 hours. God did not confer with me when He decided how long it would take the earth to make a complete spin on its axis or that a year would be measured in however much time was required for the earth to revolve around the sun. Resistance to these truths is futile. To whatever degree you choose to deny, resist, or fight universal truths is equal to the degree to which you will fail to achieve your potential.

5

Whatever time and energy you expend to change or resist the unchangeable is wasted time that you will never get back. When you acknowledge these truths, you will immediately experience more success. Embrace these truths, and you will move to a higher level of significance in life.

Why is this so important? Because truth exists whether we acknowledge it or not. I did not invent these truths any more than I had input into how many hours there are in a day or week. I have just been a diligent observer. The following list may not be a complete list of truths, but it is

a thorough analysis. What you do with this information is your choice. I simply want to introduce you to what truth is and reach an agreement on the language of truth. Jack Nicholson's character (Colonel Nathan R. Jessep) in the movie *A Few Good Men* delivered one of the most famous lines in the modern movie era, "You can't handle the truth!" I propose that life is significantly better when you choose to handle the truth.

Different Types of Truth

When someone refers to a truth or claims that some statement is true, what kind of truth are they referring to? This may seem like an odd question because we rarely think about the fact that there may be more than one type of truth out there, but there are indeed different understandings of truth for us to have. For example, the following are ten different worldviews of truth.

Empirical Truth vs. Convenient Truth

Empirical truth is based on evidence, research, and reason. Empirical truth is the truth that scientists seek. Empirical truth is the truth people seek when they want to achieve predictable results. It is a repeatable truth. Empirical truth is hard to establish because it requires a controlled set of circumstances and must be tested and observed more than once. Empirical truth can be inconvenient when it does not serve an immediate need because empirical truth requires time and testing to be established. In relation to time, empirical truth is more about past proof and future value than any present purpose. It is determined through a combination of previously established empirical truths and rigorous experimentation that other scientists may challenge before it is accepted as truth.

Convenient truth is based on need, desire, and emotion. It is the type of truth that people seek when they want to be correct but suspect they are wrong regardless of facts or evidence. In relation to time, convenient truth is about now and worries little about the past or future.

Convenient truth is the truth of populist politicians and journalists who seek to persuade without worrying about empirical truth. Convenient truth becomes perceived truth through repetition, assertion, and sheer desire. Most of us resort to convenient truth when we assert something as true when we are not really sure because it is the truth at hand. It requires little or no validation other than our desire for it to be true. We generalize from limited data or makeup "facts" to support our arguments. More often, we dally somewhere between empirical truth and convenient truth. We cannot prove every idea, so we seek trusted sources, from textbooks to online data. And we trust our friends, accepting their convenient truths as empirical truths.

Empirical truth establishes personal integrity because it is built on a provable truth. Convenient truth is a truth by persuasion, not evidence. Sometimes it is a simple assumption. When you speak truth, know what kind of truth you speak. Also, know the effect it will have in the short and long term. While a convenient truth may win the day, it may not win the war. Indeed, convenient truths can become inconvenient when they no longer hold up.

The following types of truths will help you understand different perspectives that influence individual and group action. When you recognize and consider all possible views in a situation, you will be more capable of navigating resistance when trying to share an idea through dialogue and create a free flow of conversation and action.

These worldviews of truth represent a method that provides you with a way to consider multiple perspectives and then identify the one that best fits your purpose. In any situation, there can be as many perspectives of an event as people who experience it. Using truth as a model helps you understand a situation because truth impacts perception. Different truths create different filters or different perceptions of a situation. Perception describes the way people see truth in the world.

Absolute Truth vs. Relative Truth

A truth that is defined as being absolute possesses the following qualities:

- Truth is discovered, not invented.
- Truth is transcultural: it can be conveyed across different cultures.
- Truth is unchanging: it can be altered by time.
- Beliefs cannot change a true statement, no matter how sincere one may be.

- Truth is unaffected by the attitude of the one professing it.
- Truth is knowable.

For truth to be absolute and hold these qualities, it must be grounded in a source that is personal, unchanging, and sovereign over all creation. The popular view on truth in our culture today is that objective, universal, and absolute truth is implausible. Those who hold to the idea that truth is absolute are often viewed with contempt. Postmodern relativists build their understanding of truth on the foundation of the naturalist or relative worldview. Truth then has its origin in man. This leads to conclusions that differ significantly from those who hold to absolute truth. Relativists believe:

- Truth is created, not discovered. Truth is a matter of perspective, and each culture or individual defines truth for themselves.
- Since truth is invented, there is no universal transcultural truth. Each culture or individual will define truth differently according to their background and perspective.
- Truth changes. Since truth is inseparably connected to individuals and cultures continually changing, truth perpetually

changes.

- Since truth is a matter of a group or individual's perspective, one's beliefs can change a truth statement.
- Absolute truth is not knowable. Absolute and objective truth cannot be known since it is built on the shifting foundation of man's perceptions. Since each individual's perception is different, the truth cannot be known.

Objective Truth vs. Subjective Truth

Objective truth is what exists and can be proved in the physical world (e.g., the sun moves across the sky each day). You may notice strong similarities between objective truth and empirical truth. The difference here is that empirical truths can be perceived by our senses, whereas objective truths are derived from thought processes.

Subjective truth is how the individual sees or experiences the world (e.g., today is a good day for me). Subjective truth, which is sometimes mistaken for relative truth, is a philosophical concept attributed to Danish philosopher Søren Kierkegaard (1813–1855). Kierkegaard believed that truth is a personal, not

11

impersonal, thing—that it is something we are, not something we have. Kierkegaard acknowledged objective truth as being something "outward" while believing that subjective truth is something "inward."

The idea is that, while objective truths are important, subjective truth can be more crucial to a person because it involves how a person relates to and accepts those objective truths. Kierkegaard believed that truth could not be just acknowledged, it must be appropriated; it is not just correspondence but internal commitment. Truth is found in a subjective encounter with God and acceptance of His truth by one's will, not only by an objective understanding with the mind. In other words, a person *subjects* himself inwardly to the truth.

Kierkegaard's subjective truth is essential in today's post-truth culture, which believes objective facts are less important in shaping public opinion than trying to appeal to emotions and personal beliefs. For many today, feelings and personal choices matter more than facts. Their inward beliefs override the outward facts. Outward facts or objective truth is something subjective truth holders refuse to submit to.

In a post-truth culture, people readily acknowledge an objective fact as being true. And yet, if an objective truth conflicts with personal preferences or political agendas, it is discounted in some way in favor of the subjective truth. Some people will go as far as to ignore the facts, misrepresent the truth, or even spread lies about an objective truth in order to move their subjective truth agenda forward. This approach conflicts with Kierkegaard's subjective truth concept, which by no means dismisses objective reality in favor of a person's preferences and agenda.

One of the flaws in Kierkegaard's framework is the thought that there can be a difference between objective and subjective truth. He felt that a person's faith can leave-one a state of objective uncertainty, and, because of that, faith requires a leap from disbelief to belief. However, he understood that the transition from having faith that something is true to having faith in something requires not a leap in the dark, but rather a step into the light.

Moral Objectivism vs. Moral Relativism

Moral objectivism is the view that what is right or wrong doesn't depend on what anyone thinks is right or wrong. "Moral facts" are like physical facts, which do not depend on what anyone thinks they are. They simply are. Moral objectivism asserts that there's a single set of moral standards that should be adhered to. It contends that there are rights and wrongs that are universal and that morals are not defined simply by society or the individual.

Moral Relativism is the view that morals are not absolute but are shaped by social customs and beliefs. For example, someone who claims, "Something is morally right for me to do because the people in my culture think it is right," is a moral relativist (because what is right and wrong depends on who is doing it). Proponents of this belief assert that moral judgments are true or false only relative to some particular standpoint—for instance, that of a culture or a historical period—and no viewpoint is uniquely privileged over all others.

Normative Truth vs. Complex Truth

Normative truth adherents purport that values are not determinable simply by the existence or nonexistence of things or by logic alone without reference to something further (such as the human will or objective ideals). A normative truth is held as an agreement or assumption of everyone in a group. For example, what we, as a group, agree is true (e.g., English speakers agreed to use the word "day" to name the time when the sky is lit by the sun). Tenets of faith, social norms, and jargon are all examples of normative truths. Sometimes normative truth can be implicit, like taboos or family expectations.

Complex truth recognizes the validity of these normative truths and allows you to focus on the one that is most useful at any given time. (For example: The sun is up; the day is bright. Today is a good day for Mom, so let's take advantage of that and ask for ice cream for dinner.) We use this model to help us understand different perspectives in our work with individuals, groups, teams, and organizations. As a model, complex truths represent the various truths that shape our perspective. As a method, complex truth becomes the basis for inquiry and questioning as both individuals and groups seek to identify their similarities and differences, find common ground for problem-solving and decision-making, and understand each other's perspectives and actions. It is essential to pay attention in times of disagreement because disagreement is often a result of conflicting interpretations of complex truths. You can do this by looking for cues about how people see and share their perspectives about what they are experiencing. Take time to also share your observations, which can help others gain a different perspective and possibly make sense of the situation. Using what you see and combining it with what others see can help you identify each person's unique perspective and then act wisely by choosing the evidence that fits your needs.

Feed Me the Truth

Truth is like food—it becomes part of who we are. Truth, like food, is first ingested, digested, then absorbed. Ingestion is the taking in of food. Digestion is when the food is broken down into smaller building blocks. Absorption is when those building blocks are directly absorbed into the bloodstream or lymphatic system through the intestines and then transported to various cells, tissues, and organs in the body. Our digestive systems function to ingest and digest food, absorb nutrients, and remove waste. How our body functions and operates is greatly affected by what we take in. When we eat foods that are pure or organic, our bodies function at a higher level. We see adverse effects on our bodies over time when we eat processed or artificial foods. I can easily get fast food and become full rather quickly if I am hungry. If I were to eat fast food every day, it would have a dramatically negative effect on my body over time. Why? Because I would be putting artificial food into my body. I would not be considered living a healthy lifestyle physically even though my body has food in it.

On the other hand, if I were to eat natural foods such as fruits, vegetables, and lean meats, my body would function at a much higher level. The specific fuel you give your body will determine the outcome:

positive or negative. Truth is like food. It becomes part of who we are.

Different types of truths work like different types of food. Whatever truth that's influencing us will be taken in by our five senses. The quality of truth we feed ourselves affects our mental, emotional, and spiritual health. There are real truths, and there are artificial truths. Like food, there are natural (organic truths) and processed (artificial truths). If it's true that we are what we eat, then we should be all the more careful about which truth we allow to become part of who we are.

Chapter 2
Why We Need the Truth

"In wartime, Truth is so precious that she
should always be attended
by a bodyguard of lies."
- Winston S. Churchill

"I believe that unarmed truth and
unconditional love
will have the final word in reality."
- MLK

It's been said that Adulting 101 is using Google search and watching YouTube videos. Anything you want to know or learn is literally at your fingertips. For example, I recently googled the question, "What's the difference between counterfeit and the real thing?" This is what popped up:

> To counterfeit means to imitate something authentic, with the intent to steal, destroy, or replace the original, for use in illegal transactions, or otherwise

19

to deceive individuals into believing that the fake is of equal or greater value than the real thing.

So, how do we determine what is real versus what is counterfeit? Take the cash in your wallet, for example. How do you know if that twenty-dollar bill is real or counterfeit? According to Special Agent Bruce Taylor of the Little Rock field office of the US Secret Service, most people probably have handled some counterfeit bills unknowingly in their life, especially if you work as a bank teller, a convenience store clerk, or in some other occupation that handles a lot of cash. Special Agent Taylor explained that counterfeiters struggle with duplicating US currency because the US Department of the Treasury Bureau of Engraving and Printing redesigned US currency starting in 1996 to increase security by using unique security threats, watermarks, and micro-printing around the featured portrait as well as on the embedded security threads. Each bill is also printed with color-shifting ink. For example, under special lighting, the $5 bill glows blue, the $10 bill glows orange, the $20 bill glows green, the $50 bill glows yellow, and the $100 bill glows pink. This glow makes duplication of the ink very expensive and very complicated. To further challenge counterfeiters, each bill has a unique watermark. You can see the watermark by holding the bill up to a light. The watermark is an image or pattern on paper that appears as various shades. The shading is caused by the thickness or density variations in the paper, which means it is added during the manufacturing of the paper, not during the printing. With all these security measures, counterfeiters have still found ways to make a fake bill that cannot be detected with the currency pens used by many stores. Special Agent Taylor explained that some counterfeiters use a process called "bleaching notes," using actual US bills:

> With a bleached note, they can make a one-dollar bill into a five or a twenty simply by printing a new currency image on a bleached note. Because the paper is real, the pen will not detect it as a fake. It is interesting the amount of work some people will go to in order to make something fake appear real.

I wanted to share about counterfeit versus authentic currency to show how something that is physically seen, felt, and used every day by all of us can be manipulated and used to deceive us. Social media is another daily intersection of real vs. counterfeit. How often have we gotten an email or message from a friend saying, "I've been hacked, do not send money, don't accept a friend request"? A fake account' was created based on a real account, all in the hopes of fooling people. Values and influence work the same way. Where there are real voices of influence that guide you along the path of truth, there are also counterfeit voices of influence that will lead you down the path of deception.

How can we discern which road will lead us to truth and which will lead us down the path that so easily manipulates what we believe? Our minds and hearts are easily conflicted. How can we make sure we are on the right path? We need to know the difference between well-meaning advice and sound wisdom.

Wisdom for Today

If there was ever a time that we needed wisdom, it is now. Notice I didn't say knowledge. There is a difference between knowledge and wisdom. Anyone can learn about a subject by reading, researching, and memorizing facts. Those facts don't have to be true or real for you to acquire knowledge because knowledge is more about being able to retrieve information. Google itself is loaded with knowledge. However, if we think of Google as a person, it lacks wisdom. What we need most is wisdom. What is wisdom? Having wisdom is to have insight. Wisdom is taking knowledge and combining it with experience. Google cannot create experiences for itself to test the knowledge it holds. To have a deeper understanding of certain things from personal experience and observation is wisdom. Wisdom helps us to discern the truth from falsehoods or counterfeits. In the casinos of Las Vegas, some people handle money all day long, and because of this experience can detect a counterfeit simply by its feel. Their experience has given them wisdom.

Why We Need Wisdom

We have explored why we should seek wisdom over knowledge, but what does wisdom look like, and why do we need it?

We need wisdom to know the difference between what is authentic and what is counterfeit.

Discerning what is authentic and what is counterfeit only comes through evaluated experience. Hindsight is 20/20. You don't know what you don't know. That is why deception is so powerful and illusive. Winston S. Churchill said, "The truth is incontrovertible. Malice may attack it, ignorance may deride it, but in the end, there it is."

We need wisdom to discern truth from lies.

Lies require censorship. Truth does not. A lie has speed, but truth has endurance. Truth is like the sun that drives away the thickest fog.

We need wisdom to look beyond the outside and see what is on the inside.

In society, it is no secret that we give a lot of attention to the exterior of life. You may say that people shouldn't judge a book by its cover or make assumptions based on what they see, but the truth is, we all do this at one level or another. We can't live based on how things should be. We have to meet people where they are. Wisdom enables us to see people beyond the surface and connect with them more profoundly.

We need wisdom to discern between what people say they want versus what they really need.

Henry Ford, the inventor of the Ford Model T, said, "If I had asked people what they wanted, they would have said faster horses." Sometimes the line between what we want and what we need can be fuzzy. For the purpose of this book, the question I would like to propose is not "Are our needs being met?" but rather "Who is meeting our needs?" How you answer that question will determine who you look to as your source. How our needs are met often determines who we trust and the voices we listen to.

Does It Matter What I Believe?

I often hear, "Does it matter what I believe as long as I believe in something?" Or "As long as what I believe—helps me, isn't that all that matters?" The idea behind these statements is that there is no single truth, and thus, believing in something is all that is necessary. After all, we all believe in something. As Edgar Sheffield Brightman stated in his book *A Philosophy of Religion*, "A thinker cannot divest himself of real convictions, and it is futile to pose as having none."

For all recorded history, finding truth or meaning in life has challenged modern man. We struggle to conceive of something outside ourselves. This quote from *The Rise of Scientific Philosophy* by Hans Reichenbach seems to summarize our struggle best: "There are no rules by means of which we would discover a purpose or a meaning of the universe." (, , p. 301).

Even though we live in a time in which we all have self-defined beliefs about things, the current social climate seems to place faith in the act rather than in any objective understanding of faith and beliefs. Pragmatist William James stated, "Be not afraid of life. Believe that life is worth living, and your belief will help create the fact."

The flip side of this concept is that facts don't create beliefs. Rather, facts test the legitimacy of our beliefs. Unfortunately, all too common is that our beliefs create the facts we need to uphold the beliefs we cling to.

No matter how hard you try, belief will not create facts. Truth stands independent of belief. No matter how hard I try, believing something will not make it true. For example, my kids may believe with all their hearts that we will have a snow day, ignoring the fact that we live in Texas. No matter how much they believe and talk about the pending snow day, they cannot make it snow. Belief is only as good as the object we place our trust in. If my friend who is a pilot came to me and asked me to join him as a co-pilot, I would be excited about the adventure. After all, he has a pilot's license, and I would just be along for the ride. But if I discovered that his plane hardly runs, then my faith, no matter how much I have, will not make the plane flightworthy.

My faith won't create a shiny new plane. However, if another friend of mine comes along and makes the same offer but is a certified pilot with a shiny new aircraft, then my trust has been much more reasonably placed. It doesn't matter what I believe, for my believing in something does not make it true.

We see here that it is not so much the act of belief as the object of the belief that matters. What is emphasized is not so much the one trusting, but rather the one trusted.

People seem to believe in whatever they hope for, but this random trust placement will lead to folly. We pick the truths we defend because we feel comfortable with the belief systems they construct, and they require the least amount of research to support. The truth is most people don't really want the truth. They just want constant reassurance that what they believe is the truth. Take the media for example. American journalist Dan Rather tweeted, "News anchors looking into a camera and reading a script handed down by a corporate overlord, words meant to obscure the truth not elucidate it, is not journalism. It's propaganda. It's Orwellian. A slippery slope to how despots wrest power, silence dissent, and oppress the masses." Another example I would like to point out would be the famous story of the philosopher Georg Hegel. As the story goes, Hegel was expounding on his philosophy of history regarding a particular series of events when one of his students objected to Hegel's view and replied, "But, Professor, the facts are otherwise." "So much worse for the facts," was Hegel's answer.

The Object of Belief vs. the Act of Belief

One of the darkest periods in the history of Israel occurred during the kings' time. During this time, there was a contest between the Jews' God and Baal, a highly regarded cult deity. An altar of wood was built, with pieces of oxen laid upon it as a sacrifice. The god who answered by fire and consumed the sacrifice would be acknowledged as the true god in Israel. Baal went first. If anyone could start a fire from the sky, it was Baal—the great nature god who controlled the weather. The priests of Baal paraded around the altar all morning until late afternoon, beseeching Baal to respond. These priests jumped all over the altar, cut themselves with swords, and danced into a frenzy, shouting and pleading all day. Yet nothing happened. When Elijah finished rebuilding the altar, Elijah's God answered with fire from heaven and consumed the sacrifice on the altar. The prophets of Baal were then slain, but not because they failed to start the fire. They were killed because the kings had placed their trust in them, and that trust had been betrayed. If sincerity and deep belief were enough, then these priests should have been spared. The priests of Baal were passionate in their acts of belief, but from the results (or non-results), their trust was misplaced. The priests of Baal had never taken the time to investigate the truth.

Investigate the Truth

Think of an idea once considered truth that, upon investigation, was discovered to be false. Take, for example, a common belief in the Middle Ages was the Earth was flat. However, after scientific investigation, that belief was discovered to be false. The Earth is a sphere. Scholars have known the Earth is round for thousands of years. The Greek philosopher Pythagoras first suggested the idea around 500 BC, though his thought process were driven by his idea that spheres are the perfect shape. Still, Aristotle found physical evidence backing up his predecessor's theory. By the time the first century AD rolled around, any educated Greek or Roman believed in a round planet.

When Christopher Columbus took on his voyage to the New World, the fear was that the oceans would be too big, not that he'd fall off the face of the earth. Another example of investigating the truth would be an instant replay in sports. When a referee makes a particular call, we take that call as accurate. Only after investigating the call through instant replay does a "true" call either stand or is overturned. The right or wrong call could very well have a significant determining factor in the game's outcome. How much more important is the right call in the game of life? It is evident, therefore, that there is nothing of greater importance to humanity than the investigation of truth. Today, we have the opportunity to investigate the truth and to search out our hearts' greatest desires. It's in the seeking that we find, in the asking that we receive, and in the knocking at the door of truth that it will be opened.

Knowing the voice of truth is our ultimate purpose and discovery. Truth has a voice, and the voice you trust determines the direction of your life.

Truth Has a Voice

If truth has a voice and that voice is speaking continually, then it matters not only from whom we hear the truth, but also how we hear truth. What we hear physically affects what we hear internally. There is a relationship between what we hear physically and how we live. I want to take a moment to talk about how the ear functions and how we interrupt what we hear.

Have you ever noticed that when a toddler hears their mother's voice on the phone, their faces light up as they recognize who it is? Toddlers are very hands-on and need to touch and see things in the real world to understand them, yet they recognize their mother's voice without actually seeing her face. Scientists were curious how this happens, not just for little kids but for everyone. How do we know who we are talking to on the phone simply by hearing their voice? According to an article in the *PLOS Biology* journal titled "Implicit Multisensory Associations Influence Voice Recognition," scientists examined how our brains are able to connect a person's face with that person's voice. The brain is a complex organ that has complete control over our entire body. But for now, let's focus on the parts of the brain that help us recognize people's voices and how we construct what we see.

The part of the brain that tells us about a person's voice is the auditory area, and the part that tells us about a person's face is the visual area. One-third of our brain is wired for visual processing. So, the auditory and visual parts of the brain work together to identify a person. When two senses work together like this, scientists call it "multiple sensory modalities," meaning that the two senses are so connected that they act like one.

The Physiology of Hearing

The physiology of hearing is very complex indeed and is best understood by looking at the role played by each part of our hearing system.

Sound waves, which are vibrations in the air around us, are collected by the pinna on each side of our head and are funneled into the ear canals. These sound waves make the eardrum vibrate. The eardrum is so sensitive to sound vibrations in the ear canal that it can detect even the faintest sound and replicate even the most complex sound vibration patterns. The eardrum vibrations caused by sound waves move the chain of tiny bones (the ossicles: malleus, incus, and stapes) in the middle ear, transferring the sound vibrations into the cochlea of the inner ear.

This happens because the last of the three bones in this chain, the stapes, sits in a membrane-covered window in the bony wall, which separates the middle ear from the cochlea of the inner ear. As the stapes vibrate, the cochlea fluids move in a wave-like action, stimulating the microscopically small hair cells.

Remarkably, the hair cells in the cochlea are tuned to respond to different sounds based on their pitch or frequency. High-pitched sounds stimulate hair cells in the lower part of the cochlea and low-pitched sounds stimulate hair cells in the upper part of the cochlea. What happens next is even more remarkable because when each hair cell detects the pitch or frequency of sound to which it's tuned to respond, it generates nerve impulses that travel instantaneously along the auditory nerve.

These nerve impulses follow a complicated pathway in the brainstem before arriving at the brain's hearing center, the auditory cortex. This is where the streams of nerve impulses are converted into meaningful sound. All of this happens within a tiny fraction of a second, almost instantaneously after sound waves first enter our ear canals. It is very accurate to say that we ultimately hear with our brains.

The McGurk Effect

The McGurk effect is a perceptual phenomenon that demonstrates an interaction between hearing and vision in speech perception. It occurs when there is a conflict between visual speech, meaning the movements of someone's mouth and lips, and auditory speech, which are the sounds that a person hears. And it can result in the perception of an entirely different message.

In a new study, neuroscientists at the Baylor College of Medicine in Houston attempted to offer a quantitative explanation for why the McGurk effect occurs. Baylor

College developed a computer model that was able to accurately predict when the McGurk effect should or should not occur in people. In the demonstration of the McGurk effect used in the study, a participant was asked to keep their eyes closed while listening to a video that shows a person making the sounds "ba ba ba." Then that individual is asked to open their eyes and watch the mouth of the person in the video closely, but with the sound off. Now, in the video it looks like the person is saying "ga ga ga." In the final step of the experiment, the same video is replayed, but this time the sound is on and the participant is asked to keep their eyes open. People who are sensitive to the McGurk effect will report hearing "da da da," a sound that doesn't match up with either the auditory or visual cues previously seen. That's because the brain attempts to resolve what it thinks it hears with a sound closer to what it sees.

What is the purpose of all this information about the physical ear and how we hear? Simply this: What we hear with our physical ears affects how we interpret and internalize what we hear. What we hear or what we think we hear has a significant influence on us. Just like the example in the McGurk effect, what we hear versus what is said can cause us to process conflicting messages as truth or, at the least, reality. Our thoughts and the things we internalize directly reflect what we believe. Both the physical and internal processes influence us. Everything is connected. One thing affects everything else, from the physical realm to the mental/emotional realm. We need to understand at a deeper level how the "who we are" is created. The information that we see, hear, and process affects us physically, mentally, emotionally, and spiritually. Every voice we hear influences our beliefs. A belief is a thought or an acceptance of something that is true or real without any proof. Belief is a process of the mind, not of fact. It is the process by which we trust something or someone. When we trust a belief system, it becomes faith, and when we doubt it, it becomes fear. Faith is trust that is placed in something or someone. The trust of belief is faith. The doubt of belief is fear. Influence is birthed from these two voices: The voice of faith and the voice of fear. Let's take a look at the differences between the two voices.

- Faith says, "Even if." / Fears says, "What if?"
- Faith builds up / Fear tears down
- Faith has an abundance mentality. / Fear has a scarcity mentality.
- Faith has more than enough. / Fear doesn't have enough and is not enough.
- Faith is secure. / Fear is insecure.
- Faith trusts in God. / Fear idolizes self.

- Faith motivates. / Fear manipulates.
- Faith acts. / Fear hesitates.
- Faith waits. / Fear panics.
- Faith allows. / Fear forces.
- Faith comforts. / Fear worries.
- Faith convicts. / Fear condemns.
- Faith trusts. / Fear doubts.

Be careful what you listen to. Listening is receiving, so the more you listen to something, the more you will receive it. In other words, what you listen to is processed as important and gets stored in your brain's file cabinet. So, who you listen to will influence you.

In our search for truth, our searching should be guided by our internal belief's ears, not exclusively our physical ears. It is essential for us to view life through the lenses of those beliefs that we trust. Our ears are constantly bombarded with the sounds of chaos, confusion, and conflict. Our internal ears have a completely different hearing sensitivity than our physical ears ever will. We must go beyond the surface and dig deeper. That's where the truth awaits us. That's where all the answers are. As we continue our journey, the next chapter will address the areas that identify and clarify how the most influential voices in our lives affect our acceptance of the truth.

Chapter 3
What Influences Our Acceptance of Something as Truth?

"There is no such thing as your truth.
There is the truth and your opinion."

\- Ben Shapiro

The year was 1989. As a kid in our home, we knew Friday nights meant two things for certain: Pizza and a movie. One night that I remember clearly, as usual, the pizza was on point, but that night's movie would be one I would never forget. That night I was introduced to the greatest Batman movie of all time: the one where Michael Keaton is Batman and Jack Nicholson is the Joker. You may have your opinion that there are better Batman movies, but in my humble opinion, you would be wrong. If you've never seen the 1989 Batman movie, you owe it to yourself to see it at least once. One of my favorite scenes in the movie is where the Joker is hosting a city-wide party. The scene opens with the street full of people and music playing, and the Joker is riding high atop a float. Then the float stops, and the Joker reads from his prepared speech. He is in full politician mode, as-he promises to give away free money to everyone in need. He becomes the people's savior of sorts. He was acting not out of charity but out a desire to change their perception of him, from being a villain to a hero and the benevolent protector of the city's people. Caught up in the moment, he grabs his megaphone. He begins, "And now, folks, it's time for 'Who do you trust?' Hubba, hubba, hubba! Money, money, money! Who do you trust? Me? I'm giving away free money. And where is the Batman? He's at home, washing his tights!"

In typical fashion, the Joker highlights his virtue and shames the city's self-proclaimed hometown guardian by asking, "Where is the Batman?" What a strategic question! Was the Joker implying that he was the real hero strictly because he was present, and Batman wasn't? Is a hero only a hero when we can see them? Had the people become tricked into believing the idea that someone-out of sight should also be out of mind? Is the adage really true that "The world belongs to those who show up"? The people of Gotham, over time, had come to depend on Batman as the one who watched over the city. Yet, in this moment, he was nowhere to be seen. Lured by money and accessibility, the people turned to place their trust in the one who was visible and the loudest. The people of Gotham were in desperate need of money, and that's precisely what the Joker promised to give them. They didn't realize that their trust and faith were about to be betrayed. Only moments later, the money rained down where the people had gathered, and then poisonous gas was released into the air through the Jokers' larger-than-life balloons hovering over the merriment and festivities.

When the Joker asked the people, "Who do you trust?" he was creating a belief in the people. That belief was that trust should be placed in the one who can meet your needs. The Joker was being relevant on a level equal to today's social media viral videos. His sole purpose was to become more relevant than his nemesis, Batman.

The term relevant means "to have a significant and demonstrable bearing on the matter at hand." Or, more simply put, meeting the needs of the moment. People who meet the needs of the moment will always be relevant. The people of Gotham had many needs, but money was at the top of their priority list. They believed that if someone could meet their need for money, all the other needs, like security and safety, would be taken care of as well. The Joker did meet the need, but he didn't offer to meet their needs indefinitely, nor did he offer to meet their other needs. Instead, the Joker positioned himself as a quick fix, a drug aimed at relieving surface-level pain and fears. The immediate need was money. The source was the Joker.

The important thing to recognize is that *who* meets our needs is just as important as the needs themselves being met. When we place our trust in someone to meet our needs, we have to be able to look past the need and see the person fulfilling the need as well. Quick fixes do not bring long-term solutions. In my experience, people with a scarcity mindset tend to trade the long-term vision of their life for instant gratification. Why do we do that? Why are we so willing, like the people of Gotham, to trade or abandon our trusted ally for a temporary savior that offers a "fix" and not a real solution?

Because we haven't identified our values. When we don't identify or know our core values, we often settle. Our values determine our worth. Our worth comes from knowing the truth and our identity. Our identity is often determined by those around us and their values. Those among us become our most significant influences. This book started as a self-reflection to understand truth and how that truth shaped my decisions, actions, and character. As I talked with others about what I was discovering, I realized others must also be struggling with similar questions regarding truth. So, through this book, I hope to help you answer a few questions about truth, influence, and trust. Like the people of Gotham, I

have been led to follow a few Jokers in my life, only to be betrayed. Maybe together, now that we have identified the definition of truth, we can learn to identify and trust the voices of influence that will lead us to the life we were created for, where true living begins, and away from the Jokers in our life.

The Voices Behind You: Past Influences

If I've heard it once, I've heard it a thousand times: "I told you so." I can still hear my parents' voices ringing in my ears, "Son, if you would have just listened to me, this wouldn't have happened." My dad's voice echoes from the past. I know, I know. But like most sons, I was a bit headstrong and stubborn. What is it about human nature that makes us so stubborn? Why are we so headstrong and filled with the need to figure things out our own way? What in our nature incites this need to rebel from the advice of others trying to help us? It's been said that we have two primary learning methods: First from experience and second from the experience of others. I can tell you with certainty that learning from the experience of others is the way to go. The wisdom of others is often the short path to learning. However, I have found that more times than not, I have an insatiable desire to carve my path.

41

Back to the Future

The first human recordings show that our stubborn tendency to do things our way and according to our own wisdom is part of our human nature. In the garden of Eden, God, Adam, Eve, the animals, and all the splendor and majesty of creation were in perfect union. This was the environment in which God spoke to Adam, and Adam spoke to God. Total bliss. Complete harmony. I can only imagine the amount of wonder and awe Adam and Eve experienced in the garden of Eden. Everything they would ever need or desire was freely given and available. God's voice was the only voice Adam heard. It was the lone voice Adam listened to. And then a second voice of influence arrived. The serpent was craftier than any of the other wild animals. How would the serpent gain influence in the garden? By striking up a conversation with the only other person in this story, Eve. The serpent, like Eve, saw that the fruit looked delicious, tasted even better, and gave one the ability to gain wisdom. We see that the serpent does not approach the man God had direct influence with. Instead, the serpent strikes up a conversation with Adam's soulmate, Eve.

In this pivotal conversation, notice that the serpent did not tempt Eve to steal, kill, or commit adultery; he simply tempted her to question. The serpent made Eve

question her value and her worth. Once that self-doubt was exposed, the serpent had influence. He realized that maybe Adam was too attuned to the voice of God and was being influenced so clearly by God that he would have to sneak around the side. Then he influenced Eve by stroking her ego. It's as if the serpent said to Eve, "Why are you being left out of the initial conversation?" The serpent caused Eve to question what God had said. This questioning created a domino effect in Eve's mind. *Did God really say we couldn't eat from this tree? If we eat from this tree, it will please us and give us wisdom. Does He not want us to have those things?* We see how the serpent played on Eve's insecurities.

When God spoke directly to Adam, influence was created. Adam's instructions, in reality, were leading him to freedom. The advice Eve listened to led her down a road of deception. It's interesting how influence changes from person to person. This was the serpent's goal. It's very much like the Joker's goal. He wanted to be God's equal. He wanted to be able to influence someone to the same degree that God was influencing Adam. When we are not the one being influenced directly, but those closest to us are, that has an impact on us. Because had Eve not been influenced, Adam would have never eaten from the tree of the knowledge of good and evil. It was Eve that influenced Adam, not the serpent. This is the first time in human history that the wrong influence led someone down the wrong path.

Creating our own experiences can be a good thing in and of itself but not at the expense of compromising truth. Eve questioning what God had said wasn't her downfall. It was when the questioning caused her to doubt. Questions can lead to greater belief and trust or to fear and doubt. The serpent caused Eve to believe perhaps she was missing out on something. The rest is history, or at least biblical history. Regardless, the story shows how we must be careful who we listen to and how the counterfeit voices in our life will always sell us something that our selfishness craves. When our choices do not deliver on the expectations we so confidently hold to, frustration unfolds. When we have made a mistake, we know it. When we are in the wrong, our first human instinct is to hide. We withdraw. We pull back and isolate ourselves. As a result, we are left with two primary emotions staring us right in the face: guilt and shame.

Author and professor Brené Brown has done decades of research on these topics, and here is what she had to say concerning guilt and shame:

> I believe that there is a profound difference between shame and guilt. I believe that guilt is adaptive and

helpful—it's holding something we've done or failed to do up against our values and feeling psychological discomfort.

I define shame as the intensely painful feeling or experience of believing that we are flawed and therefore unworthy of love and belonging—something we've experienced, done, or failed to do makes us unworthy of connection.

Simply put, guilt is connected to what we do. Shame is connected to who we are. One connects to the other.

Junior high school is one of the most unique times in a kid's life. You are changing from a child to a teenager. Hormones are changing and raging. Girls are obsessed with makeup, and guys desperately need deodorant. After school in the '90s, we loved to play outside for hours. A lost art of late, it seems. I vividly remember one day playing outside and exploring the nearby woods by our house. I was twelve years old when, for the first time, I ran across the torn pages of a *Playboy* magazine on the ground. Looking at those pages changed something in me. Something I couldn't understand at the time. Those pictures created such curiosity. It brought pleasure that any boy at that age isn't ready for. Those images led to movies that continued to feed the monster of what later I would understand to be pornography. At the time, I didn't give it much thought, but it sparked my continued curiosity about gazing at women whose bodies didn't belong to me. The only woman whose eyes I was meant to gaze upon would be my future wife. The initial conversation I had within myself wasn't the issue. The issue was when I decided to continue looking and looking and looking some more. I had bought into the lie that, like Eve, if it brought me pleasure, why was it so bad?

Deep inside, we all have made choices that we realized were wrong or, at best naive at that time or later. These episodes of curiosity would seem normal to some. It's no secret that teenage boys and men are hard-wired to be attracted to females. That wasn't the issue. The issue was that my pleasure was misguided and misplaced. Magazine pages in the woods were compromising the pleasure I was intended to find only in my future wife. Like Eve, I had a propensity to move towards the things we desire, even when the influence to do so lead me down a destructive path.

The issues that we face are usually not the problem. They are the symptom of something deeper beneath the surface. Every time I would look at those pictures, my inner consciousness would start shaking as if to say, *Jared, what are you doing?* Feelings of guilt would overtake me. This process all started with my thoughts. Thoughts then became words. Words then became decisions that led to actions. My actions turned into habits and my habits metamorphosed into character. The voices we allow to influence us will lead us along the road of truth or down the path of deception. If the cycle of deception is not broken quickly, our destiny will be derailed, and our lives will continue in a destructive pattern. This pattern affects not only our lives but also the lives of those closest to us. Who we listen to matters. Whether it's our parents, peers, or conversations with ourselves, the voice of influence we trust is a major determining factor in how truth is shaped in our lives.

Why Ask Why?

The late CNN television host Larry King was once asked, "What's the best interview question?" King responded that "Why?" is the most important question because you can't answer it in one word, and it forces the other person to think.

Voices of the Past

Take a moment and think about the voices from your past. You may have incredible memories of positive, life-giving words spoken over your life as a child. Maybe you are healing from a traumatic event that took place, and someone you trusted spoke into your life that allowed you to heal and gave them a level of influence. We all have both positive and negative experiences from the past. The good news is that if you suffer from a hurtful past, you can heal, get stronger, and help others. If you have fond memories of your past, you can embrace those experiences and allow them to influence who you are becoming. The past is a great teacher if you learn from it but a terrible prison if you are mastered by it. The past is an excellent place to find meaning and understanding of the things that have influenced who we are and the voices we tune into but not a place to discover who we want to become.

How we view our past determines the rest of our lives. You either learn from your own experiences, or you can learn from the experiences of others. I have found that understanding other people's stories helps me with my own. When I speak to people who have gone through unforgettable moments in life or have dealt with trauma, I am influenced by how they have come out of those circumstances. My way of thinking about my own life story begins to shift. Hearing other people's stories help me with my own because people's successes impress me, but their failures impact me. It gives me hope. I think,

If he can overcome an addiction, so can I. If she can heal from a hurtful past, so can I. Hearing people's stories positively influences who I am.

Life is a process. The ebb and flow of life feels like a dance where we do our best not to trip on our own two feet. We are constantly learning from our current circumstances and seasons of life. Recording artist and author Ricardo Sanchez once said, "Don't curse the process. The process just might be the purpose." Remember this; life doesn't happen to you. It happens for you. Every obstacle is an opportunity, and every problem is a possibility to grow and learn more about who we are and our values. You may have allowed the voice that says you've messed up so much that you are too far gone to influence your actions and beliefs. You may feel that you are unworthy of love. You may feel so depressed that all hope seems lost. Remember that our worth is influenced by the voices we listen to and trust. To move forward, you need to begin to change the loudest voice you are listening to. That voice is your own. What happened to you doesn't define you. What happens in you is more important than what happens to you.

We all make mistakes that can make us doubt ourselves and our values. It's part of life. When you do, learn to put it behind you. Make it an OLD:

1. Own it.
2. Learn from it.
3. Don't repeat it.

You've heard the saying, "Sometimes you win, sometimes you lose." Here is a better thought: Sometimes you win, and sometimes you learn. But, if you learn from your past, you never lose. Why? Because experience isn't the most powerful voice of influence. Evaluated experience is the most powerful voice of influence. This is why we need to spend time in reflection. Reflection is so essential because reflection turns experience into insight. Insight gives us wisdom, and wisdom is linked to our values.

The past is a place of reference, not a place of residence. The past is a stepping stone, not a millstone. We all have scars from the past. I was once reminded that a scar is a permanent mark on the skin caused by wound healing. Scars shouldn't remind you that you've been hurt. They should remind you that you've been healed.

So how do we learn from the influences of the past? How do we ensure that we stop listening to the Jokers in our life? It starts with guarding your self-talk. Don't believe everything you think. Don't speak everything you feel. We are today where our conversations have brought us. We will be tomorrow where our conversations take us. Start a new conversation with yourself. The more substantial influence of truth you have within yourself, the stronger the guardrails will be to help keep out the influence of the Jokers around you. Your life follows your words. You attract the life you desire by the words you speak. Your words also attract the people you surround yourself with. It's time to start spending time with people who fit your future, not your history.

The Voices in Front of You: Future Influences

Few things give us optimism for our future like hope does. We all need something to reach for, something that pulls us from where we are to where we should be. Having hope does just that. But there is a difference between optimism and hope. Optimism is the belief that things can get better.

On the other hand, hope is trust that you can improve things. Optimism is a passive voice. In contrast, hope is an active voice. I have found that I've positively influenced others the most when I have the most hope. I've also hurt and negatively influenced people the most when I've doubted my worth. Leaders who have imparted the most to me have been the ones with a clear understanding of their worth and values. Leaders who've hurt me did so seeking a sense of worth from what they could gain, not what they could give. I've been the most resilient to pain when I get clarity about who I am.

The voice of truth speaks hope to your heart. Hope is a welcoming voice. I want to encourage you to start believing in the voice of hope again. Trust that by taking one step toward your calling and purpose, you will find your true worth, and your values will become the guiding voice that influences your choices. Wherever you find yourself, be confident of this: Truth is not far away. It is right in front of you. Let go of the past so that you can reach for the future. Learn from the past but don't stare back too long.

Quit letting who you were talk you out of who you're becoming. Life moves in one direction and one direction only: Forward. Feed your hope and starve your fear. Your future is greater than your current circumstance.

Chapter 4
How Truth Is Built

"It is said with truth that every building is constructed stone by stone, and the same may be said of knowledge, extracted and compiled by many learned men, each of whom builds upon the works of those who preceded him. What one of them does not know is known to another, and little remains truly unknown if one seeks far enough."

- George R. R. Martin

My longtime friend and personal trainer, Jason Greenhaw, owns Legacy Fitness in Kingwood, Texas. Recently he wrote an article about his gym I would like to share with you:

> If you've ever been to my gym, you will notice many things. You will notice hard work, encouragement, and good music. You will see cardio equipment, weights bars and bands, and smiles (or grimaces)

on people's faces. But you will also notice two walls are made of cinder blocks. It makes a cool "warehouse" feel, but it's also a sturdy surface to throw medicine balls and heavy stuff at. Great for anger management too. I've been looking at these walls for seventeen years, and just this week, I started thinking about how these walls were built. A sheet of plywood covers a 4x8 foot area. A single brick covers 8x16 inches. To cover the area of a single sheet of plywood would require thirty-six cinder blocks. That wall was built one brick at a time, inch by inch. Success is like that brick wall, one brick at a time. Waking up early is a brick. Eating healthy is another brick. Paying off debt another brick. Time with kids, another brick. Building the life you want is a one-brick-at-a-time job. The funny thing is that brick wall can stand up to almost anything I throw at it. Had I tried to cover the same area quickly, say with plywood, the job would have been done much faster. But it would never have held up. Putting in the hard work and not

taking shortcuts is how success is built to
last. One brick at a time!

Truth, like success, is built one brick at a time. However, before any bricks are laid, you need the correct foundation. First, there is prep work for the foundation before the actual foundation is laid. Then the inspection and approval of the foundation happen before any actual construction begins. The foundation is essential to the integrity of a building. The foundation is not about holding the house above the ground but giving us a solid, stable place to build up from. I know you probably have never given this much thought to foundations. Still, it's pretty cool when you think of how much of your physical world rests on that foundation under your home and how much life happens because of that never-shifting, never-changing foundation.

The taller the building, the deeper you need to dig before setting the foundation. Why? Because beneath the loose surface deposits of soil and sand sits a layer of lithified rock, called bedrock. The bedrock is the unbroken solid rock, overlaid in most places by soil or rock fragments. Compacted under pressure, this solid layer of earth is the first building block in constructing a sturdy foundation. Without it, the building would be prone to moving and shifting with the loose topsoil. The word *bedrock* is also used to describe the main principles on which something is based, as in traditional bedrock values. Everyone is building their life on something. Everyone is betting on someone. We all build our lives on a foundation of beliefs and truths. Our life foundation matters. Our willingness to dig deep and find the bedrock of the solidly fundamental, basic, and reliable truths will determine just how high we can go.

So what foundation is your life being built on? Knowing the answer to this question is the most critical step in building truth. One thing is clear: We all need a strong foundation.

What Makes a Strong Foundation?

Let's take a minute to examine a strong foundation's characteristics. A strong foundation must follow several principles:

Permanence

It's essential for a foundation (and the building itself) to be placed in an area where it will not be affected by future construction. This is because any shift or damage in the soil around the foundation can weaken the structure and make it unstable at transferring loads from the building to the ground.

Stability and Cohesion

The foundation must be able to transfer the building load to the ground without breaking or warping under strain. In addition, the building should not be affected by settlement or any other sort of stability issues as the years go by. This allows for a much more rigid structure that can survive the natural changes of shifting ground. All points of the foundation need to be able to support the load equally.

Depth

A careful analysis of the soil and surrounding area should always be done to determine the depth of the building foundation, so that the structure can withstand shocks or stress. These include natural events, soil expansion, and building shrinkage due to seasonal changes. More than that, depth also allows bigger and taller buildings to be built and still withstand additional elements, such as wind and gravity.

Consistency

Finally, foundations must have a rigid base to fully support the entire weight of the building. Superimposed loads can cause buildings to settle if the foundation isn't built with a consistent base for support, making the building slant or tilt, and weakening its internal structure. Combining all these factors is the basics of building a foundation that can support the building and its inhabitants for a long time. I am sure you are starting to see the parallel between a building foundation and the foundation of your life and your beliefs.

As I mentioned earlier in this book, truth is not a what. Truth is a who. When it comes to our lives, the foundation on which we build our lives is always influenced by others. At some point, someone influenced us about an idea that later became a belief we built our life on. Every idea that someone at some time had influences our choices, habits, and behaviors. And as we have discussed, the level of influence someone has is proportional to how deeply we trust them. The more we trust someone, the more we allow them to influence us. That influence guides our perception of the truth. The wrong influences will lead to a shaky life foundation. The building begins to collapse when the foundation loses its integrity over time. It may not fall all at once. But slowly, over time, we will see cracks start to form until one day those cracks become gaps. If life moves at the speed of influence, then influence determines who is in the driver's seat. If life is built by influence, then influence decides the quality of the building.

The Voices Around You: Relational Influences

Three months into 2020, life as we knew it changed to such a degree that we lost understanding of what was normal. COVID-19 spurred a global pandemic that spread like wildfire. The world was placed on lockdown, mandating that only "essential workers" could leave home to go to work. In the past, our eyes would be glued to the television, waiting for updates and the latest information. Today, most of us use social media to acquire the information we need to be "in the know." We search the internet, where hundreds of thousands of websites containing information are available at the click of a button. Apps such as Facebook, Twitter, Instagram, and YouTube deliver information and opinions to the public by the second. There is a plethora of news outlets in our faces 24/7. Most if not all of these information sources are selected based on the information to fit the narrative of the host or the source. Not all information is treated equally and without bias.

What's even more mind-blowing to me is that people believe what they hear without checking the source or understanding the motive of the person delivering the information. Do we know if the source has our best interest in mind? Are they telling us the truth or telling us a portion of the truth to make that perspective or opinion believable? Actor Denzel Washington said, "If you don't read the news, you're uninformed. If you do read the news, you're misinformed."

Whatever your belief is on this topic, this much I do know: The world is on information overload while still starving for truth. We vent our frustrations and fascinations on social media while struggling to maintain a meaningful conversation face-to-face. How do we know what to trust and even more who to trust? We were made for relationships. We were created for connection. Between social media and a global lockdown, face-to-face connections weakened and for some became nonexistent. Depression, anxiety, stress, and suicides have all—skyrocketed because of loneliness and isolation. Many people have felt lost and purposeless. Author Jon Gordan was spot on when he said, "A huge increase in depression, anxiety, suicide, and violence in this country (USA) is what happens when you have a society that is focused on an external fear instead of inner peace. Tune out the voices of fear and hate. Tune in the voices of faith, hope, and love." If you feel lost, allow me to encourage you to change who you are listening to. It's not just important; it's vital to have the right voices influencing our lives. Influence is built by relationships. And influential relationships build the foundation of your life. The wrong relationships will cause gaps in your life foundation. The right connections will ensure a strong foundation from which truth can be built. The right things happen when you are in the right place at the right time with the right people. How do we truly know which relational voices to listen to and trust? I believe the following steps will significantly benefit you in building relationships that will strengthen your foundation.

1. Surround yourself with people who share your values, not just your interests.

There is a difference between seasonal friends and lifelong friends. There is also a difference between people who share hobbies such as golf, gaming, shopping, exercise, etc., and those who share core values, beliefs, vision, mission, and purpose. Think of it this way: If your primary relational influences are based on interest alone, it's like building your foundation on sand. If your primary relational influences are based on values, it's like building your foundation on a rock.

2. Surround yourself with people who produce fruit.

We all have been around people who talk the talk and those who walk the walk. There is a difference between these two types of people. Talking about what you are going to do is one thing; actually doing it is another. You are on a mission. You are on an assignment to partner with people who want to make a difference in their world. Being selective in your relationships is not selfish.

On the contrary, it's good stewardship of your life. It's like hiring the right contractor to pour the foundation for your family home. When you link arms with people who are on the same mission, it gives your life meaning and fulfillment. Like-minded people who share the same vision rarely have to be coerced and dragged into being productive. It's the difference between a duck and an eagle. A duck was made for the ground. An eagle was made for the sky. Apple co-founder Steve Jobs said, "If you are working on something exciting that you care about, you don't have to be pushed. The vision pulls you." People with vision and mission produce and contribute to their world. As American essayist Ralph Waldo Emerson asserted, "What you do speaks so loudly that I cannot hear what you say."

3. Surround yourself with people who give more than they take.

Robert Louis Stevenson said, "Don't judge each day by the harvest you reap but by the seeds you plant." The quickest way to receive is to give. Giving is living. Love isn't love until you give it away. Giving isn't just what we do—it's an intricate part of who we are. We were created for contribution. But not everyone is the same. When it comes to people's behavior, we find four primary types: adders, subtractors, multipliers, and dividers. We enjoy adders, tolerate subtractors, value multipliers, and avoid dividers. Ultimately, we should always want more for people than we want from them. So, as you build your foundation, look for adders and multipliers.

4. Surround yourself with people who listen more than they talk.

I don't know about you, but I've never learned anything by talking. I have, however, learned a lot by listening. I have found that if you don't listen to what people have to say, it won't be long before they stop talking. The foundation of knowledge, understanding, and wisdom is listening.

"One of the sincerest forms of respect is listening to what another has to say." - Bryant McGill

"Listening is an art that requires attention over talent, spirit over ego, others over self." - Dean Jackson

A warm smile and a listening ear go a long way. The truth is, most of us listen to reply when we should be listening to understand. People stop talking when they feel they're not heard. When you're around adders and multipliers, be ready to learn. Be open to understanding and allow that to become the determiner of what gets added to your foundation of truth.

5. Surround yourself with people who speak life to you, around you, and behind your back.

We all enjoy being around people who speak well of us. We enjoy even more being around people who speak well of us in front of us to other people. But what about the things people say behind our backs when we are not around? This is what we call integrity. In his book *Mere Christianity*, apologist C. S. Lewis said, "Integrity is doing the right thing, even when no one is watching." Integrity is a gift that you give to yourself. Be careful to speak well of people even when they aren't around. Speak life. Speak hope. Speak words that rebuild the torn-down places in others. Words of truth directly affect how our lives are built.

6. Surround yourself with people who know you and "no" you.

I've heard that a friend loves you just the way you are, but a mentor loves you too much to leave you the way you are. I believe that is true. What is a mentor? A mentor is a trusted teacher with whom you are safe and can confide personal issues and challenges. In a world with a significant trust deficit, finding a safe person to whom you can be accountable may take some time, but it is essential. Sometimes, your mentor will help you set up boundaries and safeguards in specific areas of your life. Accountability is a natural byproduct of mentorship. With accountability, there is safety. This takes trust on your part. Trust that your mentor has your heart and best interests in mind.

Sometimes a NO is not rejection, it's protection. Having your mentor tell you no also takes humility. I believe humility is the greatest of all virtues. The heart that is willing to hear no and still obey is the heart that can be trusted with a yes. Having a mentor, coach, or pastor is paramount in helping you grow to your maximum potential. Having a trusted voice in your life is a beautiful thing. Having several trusted voices in your life is even better. The general principle is that there is wisdom in seeking a wide range of advice from others instead of relying solely on one's own knowledge or intuition. Considering other points of view and drawing on the experience of others is prudent. Of course, twenty foolish advisers are no better than one, so the quality of counselors one seeks makes all the difference in the advice given and received.

Human beings are fallible. No one gets it right one hundred percent of the time. The wisest and most godly among us are still subject to human error. We set ourselves up for disappointment and often disaster when we build our lives, businesses, or ministries based upon the counsel of just one person. It is good to surround ourselves with trusted advisers—a multitude of counselors—realizing that even wise people can see many things differently. Having a variety of counselors is valuable because hearing varied viewpoints gives us a healthier foundation upon which to form conclusions. We make sound decisions when we have investigated the issue from many angles. Please don't allow pride to forfeit the wealth of blessing that comes from listening to the right voices. I can vividly remember moments in my life where pride deafened me from the truth, all because I chose not to listen to the counsel of my mentors. We seem attracted to the voices of those who agree with our existing beliefs. We decide to take advice from those who confirm what we wanted to hear in the first place. This is called confirmation bias. Confirmation bias occurs when we ignore new information that contradicts our existing beliefs.

Often what we want to hear is not what we need to hear. Pride is delusional because it convinces us that we are free and independent from anyone else's help or assistance. It deafens us to the advice or warnings of those around us. Humility opens the door to those around us. Trust keeps you gathered together in the room.

In addition, *who* we influence is just as important as who influences *us*. When it comes to our interactions with others, our motive should always be to want more for others than we want from others. We must be careful to motivate and not manipulate. Motivation is all about how we can help others first. Manipulation is all about how others can help us first. You must be able to communicate an attitude of selflessness to build influence and trust. As we pour into others, we become part of how their truth is constructed.

In his book *Everyone Communicates, Few Connect*, author and speaker John C. Maxwell outlines strategic questions to help you build trust, stay authentic, and maintain a strong connection with every relationship.

Three questions of truth people ask when building a solid life foundation:

1. Do you care for me?

Author Calvin Miller says that when most people listen to others speak, they silently think, I am lonely, waiting for a friend. I am weeping in want of laughter. I am sighing in search of consolation. I am a wound in search of healing. If you want to unlock my attention, you have but to convince me you want to be my friend. People don't care how much you know until they know how much you care.

2. Can you help me?

Caring for people is one thing but having the competence to help them is another. You can be sincere and be sincerely wrong. Aim to be compassionate and competent. This is where personal growth is significant. You can't give what you don't have. Competence opens the floodgates of opportunity to help others. Be a river, not a reservoir. Zig Ziglar said it best, "You can have everything in life you want if you will just help other people get what they want."

3. Can I trust you?

Trust is the foundation of every relationship. You can build trust with others if you're willing to get off your agenda, to think about others, and to try to understand who they are and what they desire. In other words, when we try to communicate, we must include:

Thought: something we know
Emotion: something we feel
Action: something we do

When I include all three components—thought, emotion, and action—my communication has conviction, passion, and credibility. The result is connection and trust. Conversely, failure to include any of the three will lead to a disconnect from people and a communication breakdown. More specifically, here's how I think the breakdown would occur if I tried to communicate without all three elements. If I try to communicate:

Something I know but do not feel, my communication is dispassionate.
Something I know but do not do, my communication is theoretical.
Something I feel but do not know, my communication is unfounded.
Something I feel but do not do, my communication is hypocritical.

Something I do but do not know, my communication is presumptuous.

Something I do but do not feel, my communication is mechanical.

Nothing can happen through you until it happens to you. Your communication must be more than just a message. It must have value. It must exude passion. It must deliver on the promise it offers to its audience. It must have the potential to change other people's lives. Connecting happens when we genuinely care, passionately help, and intentionally build trust. Connection is the deepest desire of the soul. Because of our journey together, I hope that you are one step closer to attracting healthy relationships, which lead to deeper connections. These connections will create greater influence intended to lead you to the truth. Your relationships, how you communicate with each other, and the trust that forms significantly affect your life's foundation. Relationships matter. Communication matters. Trust matters. The foundation of your life matters because that is where truth is built.

The Voices Inside You: The Influence of Self-Talk

"Until the lion learns to write, every story will glorify the hunter." - African proverb

The most important conversation you will ever have is the one you have with yourself. In her book *The Art of Talking to Yourself*, Veronika Tugaleva, says:

> How you talk to yourself decides how you feel about yourself and others. It influences the choices you make about big and little things. It determines the actions you consider essential and the ones you consider dangerous, the desires you honor and the ones you repress, the plans you make for days to come, and the lessons you learn from days gone by. Your inner conversation decides the quality of each moment in your life.

How you talk to yourself also contributes significantly to your self-image. People rarely rise above the level of their perceived self-image. How people view themselves dramatically affects how they view the world. What we truly need is a clear level of self-awareness. Awareness is a process of seeking truth. A truth seeker needs both: to know how to look and where to find the truth. It's important to note that we are not humans having a spiritual experience but rather a spirit having a human experience. We have a spirit (the living part of us), we are a soul (mind, will, and emotions), and we manifest our spirit and soul's dominant influence through our physical body. What is seen by the natural eye is temporary. What is unseen by the natural eye is eternal. That is the spirit realm. Some would call it the subconscious mind. The spirit realm is where honest conversations happen. Just as our relational conversations influence what we hear on the outside, we also have conversations that influence us on the inside. The inner conversation is the place we're going to explore. Our self-talk must lead us toward developing a solid foundation of truth. To change the road our inner conversations have led us to, we must start by redirecting our internal navigation system. We must change from within.

In his book *Man's Search for Meaning*, Viktor E. Frankl wrote, "When we are no longer able to change a situation, we are challenged to change ourselves." Not everything that is faced can be changed. But nothing can be changed until it is faced. If something doesn't challenge you, it won't change you. So how do we change from the inside out?

Change is:

- A desire: An awareness that you need to
- A decision: Learning enough that you want to
- A discipline: Hurting enough that you have to
- A departure (from the old): Receiving enough that you are able to

Changing your focus from the outside to the inside transforms every area of your life. When a building is weakened, repairs don't start at the top but on the foundation. The same is true with us. The inside is the foundation. The outer structure is built from the inside and on a foundation of truth. The result? The story of your life beautifully unfolds the closer you move in the direction of truth.

Truth Filters

We have addressed the need for change and what the process for change looks like, but why do we need to change in the first place? Because we all are prone to get stuck. Life coach and speaker Eric G. Reid said, "It takes a lot of strength to pull yourself out of stuck. Be proud of every little step you take in the right direction. Some days even getting out of bed, showering, or doing your laundry are victories worth celebrating." I believe that is true. I have experienced getting stuck in my life. I would say there's a good chance you have as well.

Life is movement. For things to change, we have to change. Change on the inside is essential because it is a sign of growth. It is the evidence that you are growing in the direction of truth. The following is a three-step process to help you navigate your truth journey.

Learn, Unlearn, Relearn Truth

To learn is to gain or acquire knowledge of or skill in something by study, experience, or being taught.

To unlearn is to discard something learned, especially false or outdated information, from one's memory.

To relearn is to learn something again.

In a way, rather than piling up information (beliefs/truths), we must be prepared to do away with (unlearn) old methods and adopt (relearn) new ones to boost growth. Lao Tzu explained it well when he said, "To attain knowledge, add things daily. To gain wisdom, remove items every day."

This process of learning, unlearning, and relearning about truth will take time, but it will be worth it. The Learn, Unlearn, Relearn method will help you make sense of what you've discovered, developed, and learned, and

was good enough for everyone else, who was I to ask for more?

It has been a long journey to *here*—*here* being understanding the final and most important truth: A TRUTH that extends beyond the laws of nature and the conditions of time and space. In this chapter, I want to share with you one final truth. This is quite possibly the only true truth. This truth of truths is infinite. This truth is not bound by time or space and is not merely subjective.

Infinite truth is just that. Infinite. Man does not create it, nor does it need man to validate its existence for it to be true. It just is…true. The infinite truth that I am speaking of is divine truth. Divine truth is infinite, not subject to the laws of nature. Infinite is defined as "unlimited or unmeasurable in extent of space, duration of time, etc.; unbounded or unlimited; boundless; endless." Divine is defined as "of or from God or a god-like power or presence." So divine truth is God's truth, which is the absolute truth about the universe and everything inside of it from the perspective of God. When I first read this definition in the dictionary and saw the words "perspective of God," I suddenly understood at a new level that I live from the perspective of me and, on some days, at my best, humanity in general. Divine truth comes from that perspective of someone or something outside of me, outside the laws of nature, outside the human experience of greed, ego, and lust. It just seems almost impossible to understand, the idea that there is a truth that was established before I had money problems or became a dad or led a worship service. Once I understood that the idea that if this truth was established before me and my questions, and yet it can still answer my questions and give me the sense of fulfillment and peace I've been looking for in trying to understand what truth is, then I realized I was on to something big. After all, the infinite, according to science, exists outside of space and time and the human condition, and it is not confined to the understanding or limits of man. Therefore, divine truth would supersede any universal claim of truth. This infinite truth goes beyond any understanding or intellect. It is above human reason and human logic. Divine truth was birthed well before any human perception of truth was identified or labeled as such. I guess you could say divine truth is the birthplace of truth.

The easiest way to think of divine truth is to imagine it as light. When we try to look fully at divine truth, it can be blinding in the intensity of thought required to understand it. I like to think of my boys and how I sneak into their room and flip on the light while shouting, "GOOD MORNING!" on school days. Before they bolt out of bed, it always takes them a minute or two for their eyes to adjust to the light. Many times, they may not want to adjust to the light and the fact that it's a school day. They pull their blankets up over their eyes and pretend the light has somehow gone away. I get it; having the light on and your dad shouting over and over "Good morning!" can be painful. But just because you pull the covers back over your head and cover your ears, the light and your dad, for that matter, will not go away just because you pulled the blanket over your eyes. Divine truth can be uncomfortable because a truth that is outside our subjective nature and our limited perspective is uncomfortable. Just because something makes you uncomfortable does not mean it doesn't have value. As much as the boys hate the dad wake-up call, it does have a purpose, aside from making me laugh.

Divine truth makes us confront something about which we've been in denial or, at best, completely unaware. Truth does have a purpose. If you have come this far with me, let us take one more step into your understanding of truth.

I established that Truth is not a what but rather a Who. Now I have said that of all the truths, divine truth is the truth of all truths. Divine truth is not simply an idea, thought, or expression of reality. Divine truth is the very essence of a divine being, which I will call God for the remainder of this explanation of divine truth. God is divine truth. God is infinite because God is outside the laws of nature. God is indisputable. God cannot be argued or debated into a box; therefore, if God is incontrovertible, His truths must also be incontrovertible.

God is not finite because a finite God would possess physical properties, which are subject to the limits of time and space and all of nature's laws. God is not affected by finite truth because He is truth. The concept is hard to fully understand, which is why I have spent so much time defining truth.

Let me try to explain it this way: If you took one cup of hot water and one cup of cold water and poured them into a glass, could you later separate the hot water from the cold water? No, it would all be the same. Divine truth is not the warm water created from all the other truths being poured together. Divine truth is more like the space between the molecules that make up the water, the glass, and the air in this example. Divine truth is not contained in the glass or defined by the temperature or volume of the liquid because those are all man-made limits and definitions. And the space between the molecules is still being discovered and defined. I know this seems like a rabbit hole of thinking, but that's what happens when you try to define the infinite.

Reasons Divine Truth Exists

"The existence of God is not subjective. He either exists, or he doesn't. It's not a matter of opinion. You can have your own opinions. But you can't have your own facts." - Ricky Gervais

Divine truth cannot be physical; otherwise, it would be like humans, contingent on our universe and unable to cause or conceive of it. Divine truth must thus be immaterial. The immaterial divine truth that conceived the universe must therefore be deduced to be:

1. Infinite, since it has no physical boundaries. If it did, it clearly would be material.
2. Eternal, since it has no temporal boundaries. If it starts, then it is contingent on what started it.
3. Omniscient, by virtue of the fact that all man knows or could know from nature and introspection is caused by it.
4. Omnipresent, by virtue of being infinite and eternal.

Omnipotent, by virtue of having unlimited power, authority, and influence.

Transcendent, by virtue of being beyond or above the range of normal or merely physical human experience.

Immanent, because God is the efficient and unseen cause of all that is in the universe, including our minds. Eliminate that cause, and the universe ceases to be and cannot possibly be.

It's essential to establish that God is not only infinite but also non-subjective. In other words, the legitimacy of God being divine truth is undistorted by emotion or personal bias. Personal experience, views, opinions, or knowledge do not shape divine truth. Instead, all those things are revealed by it.

Divine Truth Must Be Tested

The only way to know if divine truth is the absolute truth is to put it on trial. How can we know if any truth, for that matter, can stand up? We must be willing to put it to the test or, as I like to say, take it to court and look at just the facts. What makes divine truth any different from every other truth we have addressed? There are three funnels that I believe divine truth must go through to stake its legitimacy:

1. Divine truth must be tested.
2. Divine truth must be transformative.
3. Divine truth must be transcendent.

A truth that isn't tested cannot be trusted. How can truth be trusted? One must put divine truth through what I call the truth test.

First, we must ask whether divine truth has correspondence. In other words, does it correspond to reality? Second, we must ask whether divine truth has coherence. Is it logically consistent? Does it make sense? Correspondence and coherence are incontrovertible methods of establishing truth in a court of law. The four laws of logic support this view of truth:

1. The Law of Identity: Each object is identical to itself.
2. The Law of Noncontradiction: Two contradictory statements simultaneously cannot be true in the same sense.
3. The Law of the Excluded Middle: Just because two things have one thing in common does not mean they have everything in common.
4. The Law of Rational Inference: Inferences can be made from what is known to what is unknown.

So how do we unpack a worldview and see how well it corresponds with reality and coheres with our experience? We put it through the truth test.

The Truth Test

The truth test consists of three questions:

1. Logical Consistency: Does it make sense?
2. Empirical Adequacy: Is there any evidence to support what is being claimed?
3. Experiential Relevance: Does it correspond with our experiences of the world?

1. Logical Consistency

A. The Law of Thermodynamics

The Judeo-Christian teachings claims energy and mass could not possibly have originated from nothing or natural processes. It claims the origin of energy and mass was not natural but supernatural. This is harmonious with the first law of thermodynamics.

Conclusion: Therefore, the Judeo-Christian doctrine passes the truth test of logical consistency regarding the first law of thermodynamics.

B. Second Law of Thermodynamics

If the universe (this includes all possible universes) were beginning-less, we would have already reached a point of equilibrium. A finite past would have used up all of the energy in the universe long ago. The Judeo-Christian doctrine states, "All things came into being through [God], and apart from [God] nothing came into being that has come into being" (John 1:3 NASB). The Judeo-Christian doctrine also states the universe never became more ordered over time, and its available energy never increased by natural processes. The universe was created with an order by a supernatural plan but has since been winding down; thus, the Judeo-Christian faith is harmonious with the second law of thermodynamics.

Conclusion: The Judeo-Christian doctrine passes the truth test of logical consistency regarding the second law of thermodynamics.

C. Law of Cause and Effect (aka, Where did we come from?)

The universe had a start—what caused it? There are three possible answers: 1. The universe caused itself; 2. Nothing caused it; or 3. Something that is uncaused, timeless, spaceless, immaterial, personal, and very powerful caused it.

Point 1: Everything that exists has an explanation of its existence, either in the necessity of its nature or in an external cause.

Point 2: If the universe has an explanation of its existence, that explanation is God.*

Point 3: The universe exists.

Point 4: Therefore, the universe has an explanation of its existence (from points 1 and 3).

Conclusion: Therefore, the explanation of the universe's existence is God (from points 2 and 4).

*It is tempting for atheists and children to ask, "What caused God (i.e., isn't God bound by the same law of causality)?" To answer this question, consider the following:

If there is a God who created the universe, He is not the sort of thing that comes into existence. He would be outside of time (whatever caused the origin of time had to be timeless) and exist by a necessity of His nature. Think of what the universe is: all of space-time reality, including all matter and energy. It follows that if the universe has a cause for its existence, that cause must be a non-physical, immaterial being beyond space and time. Now there are only two things that could fit that description: an abstract object like a number or an unembodied mind. But abstract objects can't cause anything. That's part of what it means to be abstract. The number seven, for example, can't cause any effects. So, if there is a cause of the universe, it must be a transcendent, unembodied mind, which is what Judeo-Christians understand God to be. Furthermore, whatever caused the universe's beginning had to have the power of spontaneous choice. If we look for the universe's cause among things that can only affect other things when something else has affected it, we find ourselves in what Aristotle called an infinite regress of cause and effect. The only thing that can produce a change without something happening to it first is a free moral agent. Therefore, whatever caused the first event had the power of free action (spontaneous action). The only kind of thing that can spontaneously act is something with the power of volitional choice. Therefore, the most reasonable explanation for how the universe began is that some being that was timeless without the universe had the power of free choice and chose to start space and time (the universe) without anything causing Him to do so. Again, this is what Judeo-Christians understand God to be.

Conclusion: The Judeo-Christian doctrine passes the truth test of logical consistency regarding the question, "Where did we come from?" and stays consistent with the laws of cause and effect.

D. Laws of Logic:

The Judeo-Christian faith claims God is the grounding for the laws of logic because they reflect His nature. In other words, the Judeo-Christian doctrine states God is absolute; therefore, the laws of logic are absolute.

Point 1: If the laws of logic are absolute, then they logically infer an absolute logical being that grounds them.

Point 2: The laws of logic must be absolute because if logic is not absolute, then logic cannot be used to prove or disprove anything (the absolute denial of this premise is an affirmation of its truth).

Conclusion: Therefore, an absolute (logical) God exists.

The bottom line: The Judeo-Christian doctrine can account for the laws of logic because we believe they reflect God's nature (i.e., God is a logical being). The naturalist worldview cannot account for the laws of logic/absolutes and must borrow from the Judeo-Christian worldview to argue rationally.

Conclusion: The Judeo-Christian doctrine passes the truth test of logical consistency regarding the laws of logic.

E. DNA

Scientists agree that DNA is similar to a computer code/program or a language. Programs have *programmers*.

Point 1: All specified information (to perform a function) comes from programmers.

Point 2: DNA has specified information (to perform a function).

Conclusion: Therefore, DNA came from a programmer.

Who or what is the best explanation for the programmed DNA? You could push the

the problem back one step and say, "aliens from another planet," but the same question applies to them and their "DNA." You end up in an infinite regress until you can come to a "programmer" whose reason for existence is *not* found outside himself; this entity's reason for existence is *in* himself. This is what Judeo-Christians mean by, "God is the grounding for intelligibility, our laws of logic, and physical laws."

The empirical evidence of programmed language in DNA does provide proof of a programmer/ designer/creator of the universe. If we have good reason to believe in a creator, then we have less reason to form some outlandish conspiracy theories as to why Jesus' disciples would make up a lie about a risen Messiah that would get them killed. If God exists, then there is no good reason to be intellectually intolerant toward the miraculous (e.g., the resurrection). As the agnostic philosopher Peter Slezak said in his debate on God's existence with William Lane Craig, "For a god who is able to create the entire universe [and program our DNA], the odd resurrection would be child's play!"

Conclusion: The Judeo-Christian doctrine passes the truth test of logical consistency regarding the information in DNA.

2. Empirical Adequacy

By "empirical adequacy," we do not expect to experiment, measure, and observe (via the scientific method) God's absolute truth, beauty, personality, omniscience, omnipotence, sovereignty, holiness, righteousness, justice, love, mercy, faithfulness, patience, and perfection. In short, if you expect to observe and measure via natural or physical means an entity that by definition is supernatural (i.e., unobservable and unmeasurable), then you are demanding a logical contradiction (i.e., the impossible). However, the Judeo-Christian doctrine can be tested by examining the evidence of the birth, life, prophecies, death, and resurrection of Jesus. It can be falsified if it lacks the necessary proof or can be verified through different categories of evidence, whether historical, archaeological, scientific, or philosophical. The same cannot be said for any of the world's other major religions.

A. Admissible evidence in a court of law:

Consider the founder of Harvard Law School and his evidential test of the resurrection. Dr. Greenleaf, the Royal Professor of Law at Harvard University, was one of the greatest legal minds that ever lived. He wrote the famous legal volume entitled, *A Treatise on the Law of Evidence*, considered by many the most significant legal volume ever written. Dr. Greenleaf took his three volumes on the laws of legal evidence and applied those principles to the resurrection of Christ. After thoroughly examining the evidence for the resurrection, Dr. Greenleaf wrote a book entitled *An Examination of the Testimony of the Four Evangelists by the Rules of Evidence Administered in the Courts of Justice*. In that book, Dr. Greenleaf emphatically stated, "It was impossible that the apostles could have persisted in affirming the truths they had narrated, had not Jesus Christ not risen from the dead." Greenleaf concluded that according to the jurisdiction of legal evidence, the resurrection of Jesus Christ was the best-supported event in all of history. Not only that, but Dr. Greenleaf was also so convinced by the overwhelming evidence that he committed his life to Jesus Christ! The fact that the Christian worldview is verifiable sets it apart from all other man-made religions. This is why the co-founder of Harvard Law School could take his three volumes on the laws of legal evidence and apply those principles to the basis and grounding of Christianity: the resurrection of Christ. Could Dr. Greenleaf have applied the laws of legal evidence to Buddhism, Islam, Hinduism, Sikhism, or any other religion?

Conclusion: The four indisputable facts on which the Judeo-Christian doctrine is based—the crucifixion of Jesus, the burial of Jesus, the resurrection of Jesus, and His post-resurrection appearances—pass the truth test of empirical adequacy.

B. Prophecies of Jesus Christ as Messiah:

The Bible is full of Messianic prophecies. Mathematician Peter Stoner counted the probability of one person fulfilling even a small number of them, and he concluded that the chance of a single man fulfilling *just* 48 of the prophecies found in the Tanakh (Old Testament) would be 1 in 10^{157}! In other words, that is one followed by 157 zeros! So, how many prophecies did Jesus fulfill? Let's find out. Jesus (Yeshua in Hebrew) fulfilled not just the 48 specific Messianic prophecies, He fulfilled more than 324 individual prophecies that related to the Messiah! The first calculation was impressive enough for me. So, the probability of one man fulfilling 324 prophecies must be a number beyond comprehension for anyone.

Conclusion: The Judeo-Christian Doctrine passes the truth test of empirical adequacy.

3. Experiential Relevance

A. Good and Evil: The Judeo-Christian doctrine makes a distinction between good and evil.

The Judeo-Christian worldview takes evil and good seriously, fully acknowledging man's true nobility and cruelty. Man's nobility is real, explained by the fact that we're made in the image of God. Man has transcendent value. That's why we fumigate termites but not people, because human beings are innately more valuable than animals. Man's cruelty (his sin and true moral guilt) is real, explained by the fall. The Judeo-Christian worldview can explain coherently the solution to the problem of man's cruelty (the fall): The solution to guilt is not denial, it's forgiveness. The Judeo-Christian doctrine answer resonates with our deepest intuition about ourselves and our world. The late Ravi Zacharias, a Christian philosopher, born and raised in India, whose ancestors belonged to the highest caste of Hindu priests, said, "The Christian faith is the only faith that gives you a satisfactory strength and explanation for suffering. ... I have debated many Hindu scholars; they have never been able to answer the origin of evil."). C. S. Lewis said, "A man does not call a line crooked unless he has some idea of a straight line."

Conclusion: The Judeo-Christian doctrine passes the truth test of experiential relevance regarding good and evil.

B. The Soul:

The Judeo-Christian doctrine describes what we experience in our mind, conscience, personality, imagination, reason, humor, and emotions as our "soul." In short, our soul makes us unique and distinct from others. Notice the attributes of the soul cannot be calculated or measured. They are not physical and cannot be proven by science; however, we all acknowledge the truth of their existence because it is part of our experience. Our soul influences our choices, and our justice system acknowledges the soul (not explicitly, but implicitly). When we prosecute someone for a murder committed over ten years ago, we are not prosecuting the same physical body that committed the murder because 98 percent of all the atoms in a human body are replaced yearly. This means that when we prosecute someone for a murder committed many years ago, we are prosecuting a physically different body, but we all know we are prosecuting the same "person." How can this be? The part of every human that makes us responsible and liable for actions performed by different atoms (the physical body) is our soul. The soul is the unique "person" who committed murder and is therefore responsible. We all want murderers and rapists prosecuted for crimes committed by (technically) another body because we all intuitively know (by experience) the existence of the soul.

Conclusion: The Judeo-Christian doctrine passes the truth test of experiential relevance regarding the soul.

C. Emotions:

Emotions are types of sensations that require a mode of consciousness. Consciousness is inextricably linked to a mind. The Judeo-

Christian worldview describes God as an eternal mind. This eternal mind hard-wired humans with faculties to experience emotions like love, jealousy, pride, envy, sadness, guilt, compassion, empathy, and more. The ability to experience these emotions enriches our experience/existence and develops our character. Emotions are a real part of every human experience, and the Judeo-Christian worldview coheres with that experience.

Conclusion: The Judeo-Christian doctrine passes the truth test of experiential relevance regarding emotions.

D. The Self-Evident Truth of Human Rights:

Consider this statement found in the Declaration of Independence that is the basis for our civil rights: "We hold these truths to be self-evident, that all men are created equal, that their Creator endows them with certain unalienable Rights, that among these are Life, Liberty and the pursuit of Happiness." No worldview other than the Judeo-Christian worldview could have produced this phrase. It is simply incoherent and inconsistent with all other worldviews. The self-evident truth makes sense within the Judeo-Christian doctrine because these fundamental human rights are grounded in the fact that all humans bear the image of God. The image humans bear (our spirit) has a certain worth and dignity that sets us apart from the animal kingdom. This is why animals do not have civil rights—they are not spiritual creatures (i.e., they are not made in the image of God) and therefore are not endowed by their creator with the same unalienable rights as humans. Once again, we all recognize (experience) this self-evident truth; however, the Judeo-Christian worldview is the only worldview that coheres with that experience.

Conclusion: The Judeo-Christian doctrine passes the truth test of experiential relevance regarding the "self-evident" truth of human rights.

Summary

Here are the results of how the Judeo-Christian doctrine corresponds with reality and coheres with our experience.

- Logical consistency: Pass
- Empirical adequacy: Pass
- Experiential relevance: Pass

Divine Truth Must Be Transformative

Everyone loves a good transformation story: The ugly duckling grows into a majestic swan, the Beast is transformed into a noble prince, and Luke Skywalker becomes a Jedi master. We all love the idea of transformation. I believe we love these stories because, deep down, there are things about us that we dream about being different someday. We want our own transformation story.

The good news for us is that God specializes in transformation. He takes that which was lost and restores it. He takes that which was dead and gives it life. He takes that which had no hope and transforms the story into one of hope. The Bible teaches that personal transformation starts with divine truth. Therefore, we must always face the truth if we want to keep changing and growing.

Once we know the truth, we have to apply it to our everyday lives, using it as a guide on our transformational journey. Only by having a daily quiet time of reflection, prayer, and worship can we get to know divine truth deeper and experience the transformation we seek.

How Divine Truth Transforms

God's truth transforms lives by purifying our hearts and changing how we think about life. As our thinking changes, so does our behavior. Those who put aside selfish desires and pattern their lives after the nature of divine truth can live the fulfilling, productive life God intended for mankind and enjoy the promise and prospects of eternal life with Him. You know divine truth is transforming you when you start moving from finite truth to infinite truth. You begin to let go of finite patterns, behaviors, and thoughts and begin to embrace infinite patterns, behaviors, and habits.

Your focus turns from the outside to the inside, from the immediate to the eternal. Viewing life from finite truths is like seeing the world through different sunglass lenses. Viewing life from infinite/divine truth is seeing the world through a completely new set of eyes.

Divine truth transforms by offering:

Enlightenment, which tells us who we really are

Our prospects and personal identity encompass who we are, where we came from, and where we are going. This is valuable information influencing how we live our life on earth. Having created humankind in His image and having designed the world for our dwelling, God is uniquely positioned to teach us how to be good stewards who seek to please Him and preserve fellowship with Him. Knowing the truth about our spiritual identity and the existence of life beyond the grave is essential for us to make informed decisions and properly prepare for the future.

The meaning and purpose of life

The significance of life lies in our role as a created beings with responsibilities to the creator. We are not our own. God expects us to serve Him by living a holy life patterned after His nature. In return, as faithful children of God, we are promised an eternal reward in the spiritual realm when our physical existence ends. This gives us true meaning and purpose in life.

A path to reconciliation

While it is true that "all have sinned and fall short of the glory of God," it is also true that God loves us and wants to preserve our fellowship with Him. However, that is not an easy task. A just and righteous God cannot indiscriminately forgive disobedience and sin. To redeem humankind, He who was without sin—namely Jesus, the Son of God—willingly sacrificed Himself taking the burden for our sins in His death on the cross. This was God's plan to save all willing to trust in Jesus, His message, and His mission. Although God offers forgiveness and salvation as a gift through Jesus, we must still acknowledge and receive that gift by faith. Divine truth opens our eyes to the reality that we are not far from God. God's love has reconciled us to Himself, and that same love transforms us.

Guidance for a fulfilling life on earth

By learning how to live a holy life in a corrupt world, we model behavior that can influence others for good. This develops friendships and has a lasting impact on those around us. Furthermore, it leaves a legacy for good and brings the personal satisfaction of knowing we have made a difference.

A code of conduct defining moral and ethical behavior

What are the basic principles of moral and ethical behavior, and how do we define them? The truth that transforms has instructed us to pattern our lives after God. We are to be holy as He is holy. The truth is that we must avoid immorality, impurity, sensuality, idolatry, sorcery, enmities, strife, jealousy, outbursts of anger, disputes, dissensions, factions, envying, drunkenness, carousing, and things like these and instead embrace love, joy, peace, patience, kindness, goodness, faithfulness, gentleness, and self-control. Moreover, we find a perfect example through the life of Jesus revealed in the New Testament books of Matthew, Mark, Luke, and John.

Integrity, values, and a set of priorities for living

Armed with the truth, we need no longer be "tossed here and there by waves and carried about by every wind of doctrine, by the trickery of men, by craftiness in deceitful scheming" (Ephesians 4:14). We possess a standard of living defined through the truth of the Bible. This guides personal conduct and gives us tangible incentives for living a holy life. God is a rewarder for those who seek Him. By knowing the truth, we can prioritize the choice between physical and spiritual things properly.

A spiritual family and support network

Those who have embraced the truth of God are blessed to be a part of the body of Christ (the Church), a family of believers of many spiritual brothers and sisters who stand ready to help in all aspects of life. All of us struggle with day-to-day challenges, whether physical or spiritual. We must no longer endure mourning the loss of a loved one, illness, financial need, depression, or temptations while all alone. Instead, there is a loving community able and willing to offer help and encouragement in times of need.

Divine Truth Must Be Transcendent

To transform is to change the appearance or form of something significantly, while transcendence is to pass beyond the limits of something. Transcendent truths are those unaffected by time or space. They define the world but are not defined by the world. Transcendent truth (divine truth) is the only truth that is ultimately beyond human comprehension. It is beyond reality and is the creator of realities, existence, time, and all there is, was and is yet to be. The light that sacred texts speak of illuminates hearts with knowledge from a source beyond our visible universe.

The apostle Paul believed in transcendent truth. In his instructions to the church at Philippi, he wrote, "Do not be anxious about anything, but in every situation, by prayer and petition, with thanksgiving, present your requests to God. And the peace of God, which transcends all understanding, will guard your hearts and minds in Christ Jesus" (Philippians 4:6–7 NIV).

For God/divine truth to be transcendent means that He is outside space and time and therefore eternal and unable to be changed by forces within the universe. It is thus closely related to God's immutability and is contrasted with his immanence. What does transcendent mean? How is God transcendent? Transcendent means above, higher than, and/or independent from all others. We sometimes speak of an athlete whose abilities transcend all others. We may speak of a moment of our life that stands out as a highlight and transcends other times of life. What does it mean, however, that God is transcendent? God is transcendent because He exists above and independently from all creation. In other words, there is no other created thing that matches His power. In addition, nothing else can interfere with His power. He created all space, time, energy, and matter. Therefore, He is able to control all things.

We find this concept explained in a variety of ways.

First, God created the heavens and the earth (Genesis 1:1). Since He created all things, He holds power over creation.

Second, He is greater than all others in terms of His holiness. In Exodus 33:20 (ESV), the Lord told Moses, "You cannot see my face, for man shall not see me and live." His holiness is so great that no human can see what is beyond their physical ability.

Third, God is transcendent in terms of His sinlessness. Isaiah 64:6–7 (ESV) says, "We have all become like one who is unclean, and all our righteous deeds are like a polluted garment. We all fade like a leaf, and our iniquities, like the wind, take us away. There is no one who calls upon your name, who rouses himself to take hold of you, for you have hidden your face from us and have made us melt in the hand of our iniquities." Hebrews 4:15 tells us He was like us in all ways except that He was without sin. His sinless nature transcended all humanity.

Fourth, God is transcendent in the sense that He is eternal. No other person or thing, only God, has this property or attribute of eternality. Therefore, his eternal nature is higher than all others.

Fifth, God is transcendent in His power. He not only created all things, He is more powerful than any other thing. Job noted many of the ways God is more powerful than creation, asking, "But the thunder of his power who can understand?" (Job 26:14 ESV).

God is transcendent in many other ways as well. These five examples serve only as some of the key ways. Scripture notes that God is both above and independent from all others. God is transcendent, an attribute that should cause us to revere Him.

Divine Truth's Defining Moment

The single most significant moment in human history was the resurrection of Jesus Christ. Why is that? Because the resurrection was the fulfillment of the promise He made. This is the cornerstone of divine truth. Divine truth stands or falls with the empty grave. Why is the resurrection of Jesus important? It shows that God was able to transcend even death.

1. The resurrection proves Jesus is who He said He was.

When people asked Jesus for a sign that He was the Messiah, the only indication He would give was sign of the prophet Jonah. Jonah spent three days in the belly of a giant fish. Jesus told the crowd asking for a sign that He would spend three days in the ground. After spending three days in the grave and rising from the dead, Jesus proved His claims were valid. Jesus is the Son of God since He fulfilled all the prophecies about himself from the Old Testament.

2. The resurrection is physical.

When Jesus rose from the dead and revealed Himself to the Apostles, He had a physical body. Most people believe that only our spirit goes to heaven when we die. Paul tells us we will have imperishable, glorified bodies free from sickness. When Jesus died for us, God's plan was to transform our spirits and bodies. When we die, we take part in the redemption of the earth, a world freed from sin.

3. The resurrection is proof of transformation.

The resurrection of Christ proved the power of God to free us from our sins. We can now approach the throne of grace with the assurance that God loves and has saved us.

4. The resurrection showed Jesus had risen back to life.

Jesus appeared to five hundred people after He rose from the dead. These people spoke about this news because they were witnesses of this miracle. Some of them were killed or imprisoned for their beliefs. Nevertheless, divine truth was tested and it survived.

If the resurrection didn't happen, all the so-called witnesses were liars. What reason would people have to die for false hope? The resurrection would have to be real for them to give their lives for it.

What Does Divine Truth Mean to You?

The resurrection of Jesus Christ gives all who believe in Him the power of eternal life. John 3:16 (ESV) says, "For God so loved the world that he gave his one and only son, that whoever believes in him will not perish, but have eternal life." We have new life in Christ because of the power of God to overcome death. The resurrection of Christ provides hope for the future of the world.

I firmly believe that the resurrection proves that Jesus is the Son of God. Everything that was said about Him came to be. Including the resurrection, evidence shows Jesus transcended death. The resurrection was seen, believed, and tested and has stood the test of time. Divine truth was manifested through the resurrection. Divine truth was tested through the resurrection. The resurrection proved that divine truth can be trusted. The death, burial, and resurrection of Jesus is the physical embodiment of transformation. And finally, the resurrection proved true that divine truth is transcendent. The greatest miracle of divine truth is this: Not to follow a dead, revered teacher but rather a risen Lord that is with us. Because God was able to transcend death, He also transcended all physical limits, and thus He is with us. The influence of divine truth will lead and guide us in all our ways when we trust this absolute truth above all others.

Our personal view of God and our theology is rooted in our understanding of divine truth, shaped by our life experiences, and filtered through our character. Therefore, on this journey we call life, there is no greater need than to answer the question, "Who is God to me?"

Life is filled with probing questions. "Why am I here?" "Does my life matter?" and "Will anyone notice after I'm gone?" None of these questions can be adequately answered until we settle the question of personal theology. This process is not simple, nor should the timetable be rushed, but every one of us will do well to pursue its outcome.

I would like to offer three reservoirs from which we form our personal theology.

The *first reservoir* is fundamental. We begin with God's self-revelation. God, creator of the universe, timeless and infinite, is by definition beyond our comprehension.

In Isaiah 66:1 (NIV), we catch a glimpse of God as He declares, "Heaven is my throne, and the earth is my footstool. Where is the house you will build for me? Where will my resting place be?"

In 1 Timothy 6:16 (NIV), He is the God "who alone is immortal and who lives in unapproachable light, whom no one has seen or can see." Yet He desires to be found and known and has revealed Himself in the pages of Scripture. For this reason, no personal theology is valid apart from God's self-revelation in His Word.

Second, within Scripture, God uses various terms to help us understand His being and character.

These terms can be divided into four primary categories:

1. First are images associated with our humanness. These include God as king, judge, lawgiver, father, healer, teacher, provider, protector, and friend.

2. The second category is non-human images. These include God as our shield, fortress, and rock. He is also described as wind and breath.

3. The third category is relational terms. God describes Himself as loving, merciful, wise, gracious, forgiving, just, and righteous. Yet, while challenging to reconcile, He is also wrathful and jealous.

4. The fourth category is transcendent: The Bible says He is all-powerful, all-knowing, all-present, perfect in holiness, infinite, eternal, unchanging, and sovereign. Yet, in the perfect expression of His character, God entered time in the person of His incarnate Son, Jesus Christ—God's definitive self-revelation.

In addition to God's self-revelation, we must consider our encounters. Each of us has personal encounters with God, perhaps more often than we realize. Some years ago, a friend described Christian maturity as a measurement of time between a personal God encounter and our realization of His arrival.

Many of the images of God's self-revelation were expressed in the context of a personal encounter. It was Abraham on Mount Moriah that declared God as his provider. Throughout the text of Scripture, we find the record of intimate encounters. It is also noteworthy to realize that personal encounters often develop our faith. Ultimately our understanding of God's character is formed through personal God encounters.

The mystery of divine truth is that God, the creator of all things and infinite in nature, transcends time and space, and yet His eternal nature affords the closest of proximity to that same creation. He is infinite, yet His character expresses itself through guiding mankind in the way we should live. In other words, God is both revelatory and relatable. He created the human heart, yet lives within the human spirit. This is why divine truth is not a what but rather a who. Divine truth is not simply an idea, He is the ideal manifestation of what mankind was intended to experience.

The *third reservoir* is perhaps the most sensitive. Here we must identify our challenges and struggles.

Challenges and struggles may be rooted in our character, environment, or other factors. But, just as our personal theology is shaped by our personal experiences of God's self-revelation, we also benefit from the reassurance of God's power and compassion amid our difficulties.

While heaven is our promised home, we often misinterpret daily challenges and struggles as a sign of our failure or God's indifference. "For we are God's handiwork, created in Christ Jesus to do good works, which God prepared in advance for us to do" (Ephesians 2:10 NIV)

The most valuable pearls are formed through difficulty and pain. Jesus warned us of the challenges of the Christian walk but also promised strength and the guiding presence of the Holy Spirit. Our personal theology of divine truth is only as beneficial as it is practical and functional. We cannot proclaim God as our peace unless we can be at peace in the midst of the storm.

And so, as we conclude, I would like to encourage you with the following:

First, from the list of terms relating to God's self-revelation, select the ones that are particularly meaningful to you. These will likely be associated with some positive life encounters with God.

Next, take some time to reflect on those significant life experiences and attempt to identify the lessons learned regarding God's character in each case.

Step three involves a ruthless self-evaluation. First, identify the three or four actions or feelings that often trip you up in your relationship with God or your fellow man.

Fourth, connect the dots. For each challenge or struggle, identify the character quality of God that provides hope or strength in the midst of the storm.

Finally, summarize these thoughts into your personal theology statement. This statement will be a work in progress, just as God's work continues in each of us. But I assure you that amid trials and temptations, having your personal theology defined and close at hand is a powerful weapon over the enemy of our souls.

A Personal Invitation To Know Divine Truth

I am humbled and honored that you have taken the time to read this book. Truth be told, I am just like you. I believe we are all on a journey searching to find the truth. As the saying goes, "The truth will set you free." The problem for me was which truth.

The revelation I reached was that truth found me. It had been right in front of me the whole time. Truth was not just a thought or perspective splashed across the news. Truth is an actual person who has an identity and desires for us to discover truth for ourselves. The ultimate truth is the truth that has an eternal and lasting substance, not just something that endures for a season. Truth does not need to be headlines and commentary to be transformative. It simply needs to be eternal. And from all my studying of truth, I have only found one eternal truth: divine truth.

I pray that you have been changed and challenged to think of truth and how it guides your thoughts and decisions in a new way. This book came about because I needed to know truth and understand how easily I had accepted other people's truths as infallible. I was being led away from the simple eternal truth that transcended all other truths. I was getting caught up in defined positions and ideas as truths to build my life around while losing sight that none of these truths could stand the test required of all truths. As I explored this idea of truth, I decided to write this book as a roadmap to help you see my journey and begin your own to discover the only truth worthy of building a life on.

The choice is yours. I have presented the facts. I have done my best to provide a clear argument for the need for truth and the tools to test those truths you hold to be self-evident in your own life. Selfishly, I hope you come to the same conclusion I did. There is only one truth: the divine truth of God.

Your future awaits you. There is a joy that is set before you. With God by your side, you can walk any road, no matter how bumpy, because you stand in truth. Even in the darkest moments, listen to the voice of divine truth, and you will stay on the right path.

You will not become distracted by the temporary truths of the news headlines and social media. Ultimately, it's not what you go through that determines where you end up. It's who you listen to along the journey. When you know the voice of truth, you will discern the truth from the lies. When you know truth, you will know yourself.

When you know yourself, you add the most value to the world. Divine truth has a name, and to me, His name is Jesus. Trust His voice, and He will lead you on the most remarkable journey you will ever experience.

"You will know the truth, and the truth will set you free." - John 8:32 (NIV)

About the Author

Contemporary Christian singer/songwriter Jared Miller has been passionately leading worship for over twenty-five years. Born in Houston, Texas, Jared has been involved in music all of his life, singing at conferences since the age of eight. He has written and co-produced ten records ranging from rock bands to solo and church worship projects. He has played with the likes of Jars of Clay, DC Talk, Skillet, and Ricardo Sanchez.

That leads us to his latest venture: the book *TRUTH: The Lies We Have Been Told*, and the song "TRUTH." With this book, readers will understand the importance of finding truth in a world filled with so many false "truths" and misdirection. In his song "TRUTH," co-produced with long-time friend and award-winning artist Von Won, the listener will experience a fresh, driving fusion of hip-hop, pop, and contemporary worship that carries the message of this book to a new level.

Jared Miller brings to us a message desperately needed at this time.

Congratulations!

Congratulations on becoming a TRUTH seeker.
You are what your family, organization, and the world need most.
Now let's put this knowledge to work serving others.

To take a deep dive into *TRUTH: The Lies We've Been Told* courses, visit
http://truth.JaredMillerOffical.com

To hire Jared Miller as a coach, workshop leader, or speaker
contact Jared at
Jaredmillerofficial@gmail.com

To bring Jared to your worship team or inquire about playing *TRUTH*
as part of your worship service, contact Jared at
Jaredmillerofficial@gmail.com

For discount bulk purchases of this book for your organization or conference, please email the publisher at
Info@SkinnyBrownDogMedia.com

TRUTH: The Lies We've Been Told
is available as a mastermind and workshop

One Last Thing

Before you close this book and put it on the shelf, if you found the message of this book compelling, please consider leaving a review on Amazon.

As an author, I appreciate nothing more than reading reviews on Amazon and other book sites from those who have enjoyed the message of this book.

Your review could be what inspires someone to discover TRUTH.

Thank you